Bedtime Stories For Adults With Insomnia (2 in 1): Deep Sleep Stories& Meditations To Help You Quiet The Mind, Fall Asleep Fast& Overcome Nighttime Anxiety & Stress-Relief

By Meditation Made Effortless

Bedtime Stories For Adults Who Want To Sleep: 17 Stories And Beginners Guided Meditations For Deep Sleep, Overcoming Insomnia & Anxiety, Stress Relief & Developing Mindfulness

By Meditation Made Effortless

Table of Contents

INTRODUCTION 1

PART I: BEDTIME STORIES 2

    Japan in Blossom Season 2

    A Travel Back in Time 7

    The Ancient Oak Tree 11

    A Day in Boulders Beach 14

    Great Achievements 17

    The Golden Piano 20

    Chasing the Rainbow 24

    The Flight to London 28

PART II: GUIDED MEDITATIONS AND SELF-HYPNOSIS 31

    Relax Yourself to Sleep 31

    Barefoot in the Park – Guided Relaxing Meditation to Help You Fall Asleep 36

    Training the Mind to Sleep with Self-Hypnosis 40

    Entering Sleep – Guided Meditation 46

    The Rainy Day – Stress Relief Guided Meditation 52

    Pre-Sleep Mindfulness Practice 56

    Massage-Like Sleep Therapy 60

    Walking with the Rainbows – Guided Visualizing Sleep Mediation 63

    15-Minute Self-Hypnosis for Sleep 67

    Sliding Down to Sleep – Guided Meditation 69

CONCLUSION 72

Introduction

Another restless night? Tossing and turning for hours? You don't need a sleeping pill or a magical switch that will turn your awareness off. All you need to do is practice!

Trying too hard to fall asleep will only push that state of relaxation even further away from you. Instead of chasing your dream, why not let it get close? Work with your mind and body and allow them to set the pace in which you will shut down your senses, one by one, allowing your whole being to sink deeply into the unknown.

And with this book, you can have that served to you every single night! From eight great bedtime stories that will put you to sleep almost instantly, to five full hours of meditations and self-hypnosis that will knock down the stress and transport you through trance and equilibrium to sound sleep, this book will let you find your night peace again.

Not sure how that's possible? Pick out your story/meditation and check it out for yourself tonight!

Part I: Bedtime Stories

Japan in Blossom Season

Duration: 45 minutes

Good evening! Tonight we will travel to Japan in the spring. This relaxing story will make you feel as though you are strolling among the cherry trees yourself, admiring the blossom, letting go of worries. Please take a deep breath, find a comfortable sleeping position, close your eyes, and let me lull you to deep and relaxing sleep.

Ever since she was a little girl, Ella's biggest dream has been to visit Japan in the blossom season. You would think that a 6-year old couldn't possibly comprehend the beauty of the sakura and what these pink flowers stand for, but in her little head, that's where heaven was.

It all started with her father and a single cherry tree that was hovering over a somewhat creepy house at the end of Silkburry road. Even though the worn-out beams and ragged surface of the haunted-like mansion gave her the chills, still, she couldn't take her little blue eyes off of it. Mesmerized by the gentle pink color of the fragile flowers, she asked her father what the magical tree was. With sparkly eyes and undivided attention, she listened to her father explaining the origin and history of the tree, soaking in every single word.

Her 6th birthday was a week after she first had laid eyes on this magnificent tree, but she was still under its spell. Blowing out the candles, her mother asked if she could share the wish with them. With an innocent smile from ear to ear, Ella said: "I wished to go to Japan so I could paint hundred of beautiful pink cherry trees." Later that day, her father drew her a large sakura tree on the ceiling of her bedroom, so that the last thing she would see before closing her eyes at night would be breathtaking beauty.

Standing in front of a never-ending cherry path now, she could almost feel the peacefulness that used to lull her to sleep decades ago. Although it took her 33 years to actually visit Japan, in her heart, Ella was still that 6-year old. She was breathing in the majestic sight with the same passion, but she was no longer a kid. Her kid was right beside her, squeezing her hand tightly, not quite believing that such beauty could exist. Her daughter Margot was twelve, and she was just as at awe as anyone experiencing something so vividly real and yet unbelievable at the same time would be.

They had arrived in Kyoto the night before, and the place was just like Ella expected – jam-packed with tourists. They had warned her – fellow sakura-lovers on the internet – to find a more secluded place to marvel at the blossom. And they were probably right. It was hard to enjoy anything in the crowd. Contending with these strangers who, as it appeared, had come from all over the world, she couldn't even take a picture.

But the sight alone was more than worth it. It was true that they could have gone to a less touristy place – someplace where you could sit under a tree without being interrupted, filling your lungs with the one-of-a-kind scent that Ella has grown almost addicted to over the years. But there was a reason why she had to visit this particular place.

It was a tiny bridge over an even smaller canal that was connecting two pathways, both lined with lush cherry trees. The symmetry, angle, colors… the sight itself was more than any painter could want. But even though she wanted nothing more than to watch her daughter play with the brush and transfer this splendid sight to canvas, the breathtaking side of it was not the only thing that forced Ella into making the decision to visit this exact place.

It was the place she actually had fallen in love with 30 years ago. When she and her father came home that day, after first witnessing such beauty, he disappeared in his painting studio while Ella was doing her homework. He appeared all covered in dust, about half an hour later, holding a travel magazine in his hand. Inside, there was an article about the cherry trees in Japan, and a huge picture of the sight that she and her own daughter was staring at this moment. Even after all these years, the picture was still sitting on her bedside table. She had promised Margot that they would paint and enjoy the sight together, but it was pretty apparent that they couldn't do a thing while the crowd was elbowing them.

"Let's go back to the hotel," she said to her daughter and explained to her that they would need to find a quieter time of the day if they wanted to get some work done. Margot nodded with approval, but Ella could sense that she was slightly disappointed. She waited for months for this trip, after all.

Making their way through the crowd and out in a clearing, they headed towards their hotel. Conveniently, the place they were staying at was just a 5-minute walk away. They left the brushes and other painting tools that Margot was equipped with there, and decided that they would wake up before sunset the following day, so they could visit again when there'd be no one else admiring the view then. They also decided that they would make the most out of their day.

A few months back, when Ella was doing her due-diligence for the vacation, she learned about Maruyama park, which seemed like a great place to spend the day in. Maruyama park was sitting next to the Yasaka shrine, and it was the home of a 70-year old Sakura tree that had actually grown from a 300-year old cherry tree. Standing in front of it now, Ella noticed that there was something so different about this particular tree. Unlike all the other sakuras in the park, this cherry blossom had his branches sagging down. It was almost like the tree was weeping for its 300-year old mother. It reminded her of herself after her father's sudden death, but she brushed off the feeling immediately. Today is about strengthening the bond between her and her daughter. This trip was not only about remembering her father and cherishing the sakura memory from her childhood – it was also about giving Margot something to remember her by. Life could get busy for them, and this day, this walk among the sakuras, was definitely a breather.

The best thing about the Maruyama park, besides its awe-inspiring look, was its wide paths. That allowed Ella and Margot to walk freely, without being sandwiched between strangers.

Ella was always finding ways to make Margot laugh, creating memorable stories, making sure that her daughter always remembers her with a smile on her face. And today was no different.

During their stroll, they bumped into a group of English tourists with a guide. And since they were in obvious need of direction – Ella was surely starting to regret the decision to depend on her phone for guidance – Ella decided they tag along. At first, Margot was beginning to blush, embarrassed, but since the group was friendly and outgoing, they didn't seem to mind their presence at all. Quite the contrary – they found Margot adorable and Ella the goofy, cool mother.

And luckily for them, the group was just starting the walk, so they had the opportunity to listen from the very beginning.

"When the cool spring breeze defeats the crystal winter for good," the guide began, "these fragile cherry blossoms start blooming on the sakura trees." "Sakura, in Japanese, is the name for a cherry tree. But these aren't your usual cherries. In fact, the tiny fruits that these trees grow are not edible at all. These cherry trees grow the nation flower of Japan, which is, as we all know, the beautiful chrysanthemums."

Margot was following every single word, listening carefully with such enthusiasm that made Ella's heart melt. Looking at her daughter now, at this very moment, it was almost like staring back at her 6-year-old self, experiencing heavenly beauty for the first time.

They passed a larger group of people, all of them with their noses deep in their phones, selecting the right filter for capturing this almost-surreal view in the best way possible. The guide then made its way to a patch of clearing, offering a long and surprisingly undisturbed view of what it seemed to be hundreds of sakura trees.

"Now, this is a spot worth taking your cameras out." Thinking the same thing, Ella pulled out her old camera her father had left her. The marvelous sight sitting in front of her was already polished to perfection by nature, but Ella wanted more. She wanted to make sure that every single detail would be just idyllic. So she took her time adjusting, balancing, ensuring the perfect level before making the snap. Snap, snap, snap. She took many pictures, most of them with Margot in the background. Their joy and satisfaction at that moment were easy to see to anyone who passed them by in Maruyama Park that day.

When they finally came out of their happy bubble, they have noticed that the group was gone. "It couldn't have been that long" Ella said. Margot just giggled, thinking how silly her mather could be some times. "There," she showed her, "they have not gone too far, *mother*." Oh how she loved to call her *mother*. Ella made a goofy face to express her pretend annoyance, but secretly, she adored that word. Mother. What a profoundly accomplishing thing that was to her.

"…so there are different meanings behind the sakura blossom," the guide was explaining to the group when they returned. "They obviously represent the arrival of warmer, more vivid times, as spring rolls over, but they also have a hidden meaning that not everyone knows. Cherry tree blossoms last for a really short time. The timetable of blooming is different in different parts of Japan., but they usually take a week to reach full bloom. And in the next five days, their petals start to fall."

Of course, Ella was well aware of all facts considering the magnificent sakura trees; Nevertheless, she was still captivated by what the guide was saying as if she was hearing these facts for the very first time.

"To Japan, the fragility of their existence is the same as our time on this earth. To the Japanese people, the short beauty of cherry blossoms represents life itself. The flowers may offer renewal when winter takes off, but they are also an annual reminder for us to appreciate life more, as it is only temporary and often too short even." The guide's words hit Ella hard, as she, once again, remembered her father and his short life. She was reminded of how fragile he, too, was at the end, just like the sakura trees, letting go of their gentle pink petals, so they could finally be free and hit the ground.

"Let's go. We don't want to waste the whole day touring around the park. Let's have some fun," Ella said to her daughter, and Margo nodded in approval as she was getting pretty hungry and tired.

Thankfully, there was an enticing aroma of street food coming from every corner of Kyoto at this time of the year. They grabbed something to eat and decided to make a picnic below a sakura tree, admiring the sunset and all the mesmerizing beauty that was surrounding them.

Back at the hotel, they barely managed to kick their shoes off. They were so tired; they passed out into a deep sleep almost immediately.

As agreed, their alarm forced them out of bed early the next day. The sun was not out yet, which was perfect for what they had on their agenda. Ella loaded her rucksack with paint, brushes, and everything she needed for painting the idyllic view from the small bridge over the canal. Still feeling sleepy, they shut the door behind them and headed out.

Just as Ella predicted, all was quiet this early in Kyoto. They had just five minutes to get to the spot, so they could afford to make a small detour to grab something to eat from a 24-hour open bakery that was just around the corner. Margot's work could take hours, and they needed to put something in their system to keep them going.

When they finally arrived at Ella's dreamy spot, the pathways were empty. There were no tourists passing by, no people admiring the beauty that was all around them. Just them two and the sakura trees.

When Margot finally assembled her portable atelier, the sun was slowly to beginning to peek through the sakura branches, illuminating the pink petals, giving more life to the painting. Ella was sitting next to Margot, watching the brush strokes carefully, admiring her talent. Although this was Ella's dream when she was a kid – to come to Japan and paint the sakura trees – unfortunately, she didn't move past her childish drawings. The painter's talent of her father had skipped a generation. She was artistic with the camera, but that was about it. But even though she couldn't transport the beauty in front of her to canvas, she couldn't be happier that her daughter could do that for her. She had great things in front of her, Margot, and Ella was ready to do all in her power to make sure heer dreams came true.

Both of them were so mesmerized by what they were experiencing, that they barely noticed the group of tourists standing next to them, admiring Margot's talent. Many hours had passed when Margot finally finished the painting, but there was no better way to spend the morning.

Speechless and completely at awe by how her daughter was able to recreate the scene so vividly, Ella began to cry. Looking at her daughter now, she couldn't help but think of the resemblance she shared with her late grandfather. Although her father was long gone now, Ella could somehow feel his presence. His deep ocean-blue eyes still pointed in her direction, watching over her from above, sharing this moment with her.

Her dream had finally come true.

A Travel Back in Time

Duration: 45 minutes

Good Evening! Tonight, I will take you on a journey that will transport you back in time. So, settle comfortably, turn off your electronics, close your eyes, and let this mesmerizing story allow you to drift off peacefully.

It was a rainy day when she got the call. Isobel had been waiting for this job offer for months, and finally, they called to let her know their decision – she got it. She was doing fine designing clothes and selling them in her father's shop in their small town, but she wanted more from her life. She wanted to be recognized, her work to be respected. And this opportunity was her ticket that would lead her there.

Her happiness could be detected from miles away. She was wearing a huge smile across her face that was simply impossible to hide. And why should she? It was how she was feeling after all. But her smile suddenly turned upside down, when the words finally hit her – "We expect you to start as soon as possible – ideally next week." They had an important fashion show coming real soon, and they were one designer short. This meant that Isobell would be an essential asset to them during this busy time. This filled her with such thrill that her chest almost started to hurt, but there was something else that was causing that pain, and it wasn't happiness. She had to make the transition in the following days. That meant telling her poor father that she was about to leave him all alone so she could go chase her big dreams. She knew that he would be happy for her, but she also knew that the news would devastate him on the inside.

But she had no time to waste if she was to start working for this widely recognized brand the following week. So she gathered the courage and spilled the beans over dinner. Her father was so happy for her and understanding, that she spent the entire evening crying, both from happiness and sadness at the same time.

In just three days, everything was ready for her to leave. She packed her bags, loaded her small red Toyota, kissed her father goodby, and headed off. It was raining just as heavily as the day she got the call. Her father had warned her to postpone the departure, to wait for the weather to clear – he was obviously being protective and worried. But she didn't want to waste a second. She told him that all would be well and that she'd call him from her new place.

She had over 10 hours to drive, and she knew that she would have to make a long stop on the way, to at least take a nap and rest. So she really had no time to waste. It was 4 AM – she wanted to skip the rush hour and wanted to make sure she'd really be there by 8 PM, as that's when they were expecting her to arrive.

As she was passing by the usually busy streets, she couldn't help but notice how peaceful her town looked this early, even with the summer rain pouring heavily. The wipers worked without stopping, but still, the road was barely visible. But she kept going, as had a pretty good reason to keep herself together and focused on her goal – which was meeting with her superior later that night.

She needed to slow down significantly, and after only two hours on the road, she already started to regret not listening to her father. "Why didn't I called to let them know I couldn't make it today?" she thought as she was trying to make her way through the jam-packed road. Apparently, there was some accident ahead that caused a total collapse on her side of the road. That only added to her anxious feelings, as she was a decent driver, but still, when it came to driving in such weather, her confidence was not very high.

It was raining for four days straight, so leaving earlier wasn't a better option either. All she had to do was just sit in her car and wait for the busy road to clear. But It had been an hour and she had barely moved a mile. So, she took her phone and started searching for an alternative route. She saw that there was a small road on the right, about 1/3 mile ahead, so she decided to take it.

Fifteen minutes later, when she was finally there, she noticed that she wasn't the only one who thought of rerouting. But it wasn't too bad. At least she could speed up and drive more freely. Of course, she wasn't really sure where the way would lead her – she had never been in this part of the county. Plus, the road was barely visible on the map – it was too narrow and pretty insignificant – there was really nothing there. But since all roads lead somewhere, she thought this was a better way to reach the highway than crawling onto the one that she had been on earlier. After all, she had seen that she should turn right 15 miles ahead, and then after 30 miles or so, the next road will connect with the highway.

But the rain was pouring as if she was standing under a waterfall. It was so heavy that she could barely even drive straight – she couldn't possibly fiddle with the map at this point. And since there was no place where she could pull over safely, she decided to just keep going. She surely remembered when and where to turn right.

But 20 miles passed, and the turning point was nowhere to be seen. "Have I really missed it?" she wondered. She knew it could be possible since the visibility wasn't all that great, and to be fair, she really was in the middle of nowhere. She had no other choice than to drive ahead and find a clearing where she could pull over and check the map again.

Three miles ahead, she parked her car alongside the road. It was still raining, but it wasn't as heavy as before. If only she had started her journey a couple of hours later. But she knew that no good could come out of dwelling on it, so she took her phone to see where she was. Nowhere. She. Was. Absolutely. Nowhere. There was no signal, no connection. She couldn't open the map, and her offline version didn't even show this road. Oh, how she missed the old analog times. Things had been a lot easier with paper maps. Weren't they?

But the rain was getting tired, and that was a good sign. At least she could see where she was headed. And with the sun peeking through the clouds, the morning was starting to get noticeable.

"Okay, calm down, relax. Just drive. You will arrive on time. It's okay" she whispered the words for consolation, and with her hand on the keys, she tried to start the car. Tried, not succeeded. Because she couldn't turn it on. After 20 minutes of trying, yelling, punching the wheel, she decided that she should look for help. She transferred all of her important things into a smaller bag – it wasn't safe to leave all of her belongings in the car in the middle of nowhere. Her laptop, wallet, documents, jewelry, and a change of clothes in case she got soaked was all she took.

And she did get soaked. After only 5 minutes of walking, the rain got angrier again – falling heavily onto her clothes, they got completely drenched. But she had to keep moving forward. She knew that she couldn't afford to wait for the rain to pass in her car and waste precious hours. She had to find help – someone who could fix her car so she could be on her way to her new home.

But there was nothing ahead but the sound of the weighty rain, hitting the asphalt. A weird sensation took over her as she noticed that there was absolutely no one passing through. No cars, no people… There were no houses in her sight, and she was starting to feel a little bit unsettled. It was daylight, that was a good start, but still, she was beginning to get scared.

15 minutes passed, and the rain finally stopped. She was looking for some shelter to change her clothes, but there was nothing but trees in the distance. Just as she was about to head toward an old oak tree and change, a carriage passed her way. "How strange," she thought. The people on the carriage didn't seem to notice her, so she continued walking toward the tree. But after only seconds, a second carriage appeared. She noticed that the people were dressed differently. Being a designer, the clothes were the first thing she noticed – it was a professional habit of hers. But even that didn't strike her as particularly odd, until yet another carriage appeared, this one, going in the opposite direction.

The two carriages pulled to a stop so the people could greet each other. They talked briefly about the heavy rain and the possible damages to their crops. She noticed that the people in the other carriage wore similar clothes. It was strange, but not unbelievable, surely. She loved time-traveling stories, but she was a rational person – there had to be an explanation as to why she saw no car driving down this road, and why the only thing that was there were three carriages and people wearing century-old clothes.

Hiding behind the tree, she managed to change her clothes without being seen. Or at least she thought so. Because the second she emerged, she saw a woman and a small child staring as if they had been waiting for her.

"Hello", the woman greeted her. "We saw a car about half a mile back, is it yours?" she asked. "Yes, it is The truth is, I am lost. I took a wrong turn, so I stopped to check the map, but there was no signal. Even more conveniently, my car wouldn't start. I started walking to see if I could find someone to help me out, but I got soaked. That's what I was doing behind the tree – changing my clothes." Isobell explained.

"You poor thing," the woman said, "come with us. Our town is just a couple of miles ahead, we are headed there now. We were stranded in another village, so I have to check if everything's okay back home. After that, I'm sure my husband will be happy to transfer you to another town close-by, where there are actual cars and mechanics." The woman laughed.

It was all starting to get clear now. Although not so sure how she could get lost this deep in the Amish county, everything made sense now. The carriages, the clothes, the absence of cars. She knew that this meant that she would need at least a couple of hours to get to the town, but what other choice she had.

She thanked the woman and hopped onto the carriage. It was strange to her how happy and content these strangers were. A life without anything digital in it? She wasn't sure if she could last a day without her phone, but she understood why other people chose to live that way. It was more than just a religion. It was about finding true values and teaching them to next generations.

When they finally arrived at the town, and after the woman explained to her husband and he agreed to take Isobell back to her side of the country, it all became clearer. These people didn't need gadgets, features, or anything other than the absolutely necessary. It was pure and unpolluted. That's how she perceived their lifestyle.

Just as she predicted, two hours had passed when she finally reached the town. It was a tranquil little place that was filled with small-town charm she knew too well. The place she grew up in was just as splendid. The mechanic's shop was sitting at the end of a small street, below a blue-sided house which also happened to be his home. He was too kind and offered to drive her to her car, and then tow her back to the town, from where she could catch the next train.

She called her superiors to let them know she was running late and wouldn't arrive before 1 AM. She was surprised to hear how polite and understanding they were, agreeing to see her the next morning and telling her where to get the keys to her new apartment. Her new home. She was so looking forward to living alone. Ever since her mother passed, it was just the two of them – Isobell and her father. But at 25, she knew it was time for her to leave the nest and find her own place in this world. This thought filled her with feelings of joy and content, and all of her troubles from earlier vanished. She had regained her confidence and was beginning to feel good again.

She agreed with the mechanic to return to her car on the weekend, and greeted him goodbye. The train station was only a few minutes away, so she didn't have to rush. She bought the ticket, and after 10 minutes, the train arrived. She found an empty seat by the window and seated comfortably.

Although she was clearly excited about her new beginning, the butterflies in her stomach were no longer there. Instead, all she could think about was the kind Amish people she met earlier that day. She was thinking about their town, their community, the children, their lifestyle… Again, as a designer, she put her focus on their clothes. How simple, traditional, and beautiful they were. Today was a real eye-opener for her. She met simplicity in a way she didn't think existed. That inspired her to think about a new line of clothing – something simple, but still strikingly beautiful.

She rested her head onto the window, closed her eyes, and lines, cuts, sketches found their way into her mind. Today was not a day to remember by the bad things that happened. Because, in the end, it didn't feel like she got lost. The whole experience seemed more like a travel back in time. Something that inspires, and that should be appreciated!

The Ancient Oak Tree

Duration: 30 minutes

Find a comfortable sleeping position and close your eyes. Allow me to tell you a story about a man, visiting his favorite spot from his childhood – sitting on the meadow, in the shadows of the ancient oak tree. Listen carefully to the sound of my voice, and allow the words of this story to put you in a relaxing and sleepy mood.

To him, the meadow had never looked that beautiful. There was something about its vibrant colors that gave him a feeling of nostalgia that was so deep, he was about to shed a tear. Blue, yellow, and red flowers laid all across the lush green blanket, and colorful butterflies danced around them so beautifully, the sight was almost too dreamy to be true.

But it was true; he knew that too well. It wasn't the first time he stood there admiring the striking beauty that nature had. When Adam was a kid, he used to come here every weekend with his mother. She would pack cucumber sandwiches and her irresistible strawberry pound cake, and they would spend long hours laying down and playing in this exact spot that he and his daughter were now seated.

From under this ancient oak tree, everything looked peaceful. Adam wasn't quite sure exactly how old the oak was, but he remembered his mother telling him that it had endured at least a couple of centuries. Surviving wars, earthquakes, floods, the tree was still standing tall, providing shelter from the sun, allowing a sight breeze to cool off the hot summer afternoons. Although it wasn't summer yet, he still remembered how hot the weather used to get in mid-July, and just how relieving the oak shadow was on those days.

Adam remembered the story about his grandfather – his mother's father – and how he managed to survive a German attack while hiding behind an old oak tree on this side of the mountain. As a kid, he loved to pretend that it was this very tree that had saved his grandfather's life. Of course, even as an 8-year-old, he knew that it was very unlikely. There were many old oak trees in this part of the woods, so the chances were pretty skim. Nonetheless, he used to sit here as a child, picturing his grandfather in his warm uniform, spending a couple of days hiding behind this tree, immobile and silent. Enduring whatever had been necessary to survive World War II.

When he was a kid, his grandmother used to keep a framed picture of his grandpapa in his soldier days – dressed in his pilot uniform, standing proudly tall that he was just about to take off to play his part in saving the world from evil. He remembered those days spent on Nana's lap, listening to stories of bravery and victory, wishing that one day, he could be a real hero just like grandpapa. Because in his eyes, his grandfather had always been a hero.

Sitting under the same oak tree, now, 35 years later, Adam couldn't help but notice that same feeling took over him, floating through his veins, announcing their presence in his mind. Even though he grew older and wiser, deep down, he was still that 8-year-old.

A smile took over his face as he realized that even decades couldn't wash away the deep sensations that we discover in our early childhood. He kissed his daughter gently on the head and hoped that she, too, was developing such emotions – a deep connection that would have today's memory engraved in her brain. He wished that when she got older, she would also be able to re-discover and still cherish these sensations even after any years. He was proud of that thought. Proud to be able to share this moment with his beautiful daughter, just like he used to enjoy those times under this oak tree with his mother.

Thirty-five long years had passed, but still, the places remained unchanged. Everything was just like Adam remembered – the smell, the grass, even the butterflies looked the same. And yet, he couldn't find what he was looking for. There was a river just a minute walk away, so he knew that it was possible for heavy rains to had caused a flood. That would surely wash away the ground below the oak tree, and with that, the contents buried not too deep underneath the upper layer. After all, he was just eight years old when he did it.

The idea came from one of his grandmother's stories. She used to tell him how soldiers used to stuff smaller caskets with cans of food, socks, and weapons, and bury them into the woods. They used to do this so that their stranded fellow soldiers could find them in cases of emergency. They had special marks for those places – secret signs that the Germans couldn't possibly notice. And even if they did, they would never know where to dig or what to look for. Exciting and adventurous, this gave little Adam an idea to do the very same thing.

These war stories, although made him proud to be on the winning side, also scared him. He was surely proud of his grandpapa and all his achievements, but still, there was something unnerving about all of that. "What if the Germans come back?" he used to ask his grandma. And even though she gave a proper answer as to why that was unlikely and explained how things don't function that way -There cannot be an invasion without at least a head's up, first, Adam was still not convinced.

So he did what those soldiers used to do during WWII. He used up all of his month's allowance to buy some canned beans, peas, and tuna. He grabbed an old map, a flashlight, a couple of pairs of batteries, and packed them all in a Ziploc bag. Then, he placed the plastic bag into a wooden box, grabbed the little shovel from their garage, took his bike, and rode towards the ancient oak tree.

When he finally got to the meadow, little Adam spent a couple of hours looking for a place to bury what he considered to be a real treasure. Once he found a soft spot about 10 feet away from the oak tree, he dug a hole that was not very deep and buried the box not that far from the upper layer of the ground. Then, to mark where his treasure was, he carved and X into the bark lower part of the bark of the oak. That way he would know – all he would need to do is stand in front of the X, then count 10 feet in that direction, and that's where his treasure was.

Even after all of these years, Adam remembered this very well. The X sign, the distance between the box and the oak tree, and yet he couldn't find it. Thirty-five years had passed, many seasons had changed, the tree was older, so it was obvious that it had endured more tough times. And he knew, he was only 8 years old. How deep into the bark could he had craved the sign?

Just as he was getting disappointed, it hit him. He remembered that a black bird, a raven perhaps, was staring at him creepily that day. And the bird was holding onto a branch of another huge tree. So, he looked around to find the largest tree in his surrounding. When he finally did, he counted 10 feet in that direction, and started digging.

It didn't take long, really. As soon as the shovel sunk into the ground, he heard the sound he was waiting for all along. The box was starting to fall apart, but the bag was still in good condition. He was surprised even to find it, considering that it wasn't deep into the ground. What surprised him even more was the condition the bag was in. The map was undamaged, the cans just like they came straight from the store.

When his daughter asked him what that was, he told her all about the war stories his grandmother used to tell him, and how that made him do something in case of an invasion. He wanted to be a hero, just like his grandfather.

His daughter was older than he was when he buried the box - she was eleven and already understood things more clearly, so he was glad he got to do this with her. He saw the spark in her eyes and how exciting this whole thing was to her, and he appreciated this moment deeply. He kissed her on her cheeked, held her hand tightly, and wished that this inspired her to create a memory of her own – something that she would later re-discover with a kid of her own. Because there was no greater happiness than being able to share a moment like that with your child.

A Day in Boulders Beach

Duration: 30 minutes

If you like doing adventurous things and visiting one-of-a-kind places, then you will truly enjoy this story. Tonight I am taking you to Boulders Beach – an African beach like no other. A beach where you can swim together with the penguins. So, keep that thought in your head, find a comfortable sleeping position, make sure you will not be disturbed, close your eyes, and get ready to drift off.

Situated on False Bay, between Simon's Town and Cape Point, lies a beach like no other. Located in the Cape Peninsula, near the great Cape Town, there is a beach called Boulder's beach. If you were to go swimming there three decades ago, you wouldn't have found anything that interesting. Of course, you would still have a great time as the clear water and sandy beach were hard to resist. But as impressive as that is, it cannot quite compare to why the beach is so famous today. For three decades, Boulders Beach has been popular thanks to its unusual residents – the cute penguins.

For almost 30 years, African penguins have been living among the boulders, cooling off in the clear water in the False Bay. Although these incredible African penguins are considered to be an endangered species, at Boulders Beach, they are safe and sound. The beach is a part of the Table Mountain National Park, and it is secured at all times. There are special regulations and rules that visitors must stick to, to ensure a safe and healthy environment for the cute inhabitants.

It all started in 1982 when two breeding pairs of penguins settled on the beach. These birds, even though they are vulnerable and about to be extinct. What pleases the animal lovers, though, is that the pair of penguins have managed to grow into over 3,000 birds the last years.

When Tim first heard about this amazing beach, he knew that he had to visit South Africa and spend some time among the African penguins. After two years, he was able to plan his trip well.

With only a backpack and a will to explore, he arrived at the Cape Town airport at 8 AM that morning. He was aware that, since it was a hot day, the beach would be packed. After all, everyone advised him – even the Cape Town travel guide warned to come early. But this was the only affordable flight available, so he had no option. He could have left the trip to the beach for the following day, but he had other things planned, and he couldn't afford spending the night in Cape Town. So, with no time to waste, Tim found transport to Cape Town's train station.

On his commute to Simon's Town, Tim couldn't help but take multiple photos of his scenic ride. The train passed along the coastline of Kalk Bay, which offered a magnificent view that had him thinking he was almost dreaming. The long shore was allowing the commuters a peek into the idyllic beauty that the South African nature had in this part of the country. While on the train, he began to explore his options. There were a couple of ways to reach the Boulders Beach from Simon's Town train station – to catch a taxi or take a walk there. Since he wanted to be wise about spending his money, he decided on the latter. And that's what he did.

Once the train pulled to a stop, Tim took out his map to check which direction he should head in. He estimated that it would take him about half an hour to get there, so that didn't seem that bad. But as soon as he started walking, he started to regret his decision. It was a really hot day, and he was drenched in sweat after 10 minutes of walking. But the thought of walking and swimming among these incredible birds gave him the motivation to keep walking.

When he finally saw the Boulders Beach sign, it was almost like a cool breeze took over him, cooling him down, congratulating him for finally getting there. The line in the Boulders Visitor Centre was not as long as he thought it would be, so that indicated that the beach would not be jam-packed with tourists after all. Which was, obviously, a good thing, as Tim was looking forward to capturing a day in the life of these cute inhabitants, without tourists peeking from every corner.

Once he paid the conservation fee, they showed him the pathway that he was supposed to pass through to get to the boulders and get near the African penguins. The wooden deck and railing were sitting beautifully above the beach, so he had to stop and take a few photos. From his perspective, there were not many people admiring the birds today, so that caused a smile on his face.

When he finally got there, he was absolutely at awe. He had seen many photos, read multiple articles, and watched a lot of videos regarding this one-of-a-kind beach, but when he was finally facing these black-and-white birds in person, he was speechless. He had been standing still for at least several minutes when a penguin from behind him made a sound that startled him. If it wasn't for this goofy bird, who knows how long would he be standing in that same position, without making a move or sound.

Boulders beach was just as he expected, if not even more striking. The granite boulders had created a sheltered home for these beautiful birds, and it was clear to every visitor that the place was maintained up to very high standards.

It was almost surreal what the place looked like. Although it was set in the middle of what seemed to be a residential area – Tim could easily spot at least a couple of dozen houses that overlooked this beach – it was a place where you could practically swim along with these endangered birds. Observing from an incredibly close range, Tim was tempted to pet one of these black-and-white animals, but he resisted that urge. Even though they were unbelievable cute, Tim remembered that these penguins were wild animals, after all; as such, they could be extremely unpredictable. There was even a sign warning the visitors not to feed the animals nor come too close to them.

He put down his backpack and took out his towel. He laid the camera below his shirt, protected from direct sunlight, and headed toward the water. He couldn't possibly be visiting this beach and miss the chance to actually swim near the penguins – he would be crazy to pass on that opportunity.

He found a spot that was not crowded, and headed there. The water was cooler than he thought it would be, which was relieving given his hot 30-minute walk here. He was not really swimming, as he was afraid that he might scare the penguins away – he was more sitting in the shallow part of the sea, observing the beautiful birds, admiring the sight and appreciating he had managed to take the trip.

Sitting there, he noticed that the penguins do not show signs of being intimidated by his presence, so he thought that it would be wise to get his camera and try to take some raw photos there.

Tim went back for his camera and gently headed toward the same part of the sea, minding his steps and walking slowly and carefully so that he wouldn't scare the birds away. His tactic was not to move, but allow the penguins to come near him themselves. He was very patient and clicked on his camera only when absolutely sure about the snapshots. To his surprise, he took some great photos.

When he got out of the water, he spent the next couple of hours just sitting on the beach and really breathing in what was happening around him. Even after 3 hours, the place looked just as awe-inspiring as the minute he got there. He thought about all of those houses up the hill that overlooked the beach. If it was his house with the most spectacular view in the world, he would spend his morning on the balcony, sipping coffee, observing these vulnerable birds, and admiring the dreamy sight every single day.

After a while, the time to leave Boulders beach rolled in. Although Tim would rather make a camp and spend the night there, he knew that he had to go. Sad to leave but content to had spent such an amazing day in one of most beautiful places on earth, he took a final look at the black-and-white birds sitting lazily on the boulders and started walking away.

Later, on the train back to the airport, he wasn't observing the magnificent views out of the window like last time. Now, Tim was eagerly scrolling through the photos he took that day. Although he loved them all dearly, it wasn't too hard to pick a favorite. The absolute winner was a penguin swimming in his direction; its eyes pointed at the camera as if it knew that a photo was being taken. He knew, at that moment, that this magazine-worthy penguin photo would be framed in his bedroom, so that he could always remember the day he spent among the African penguins.

Great Achievements

Duration: 30 minutes

Lie down in your bed, wearing comfortable clothes, and settling into a position that does not irritate you. Close your eyes, and let my words lull you to sleep. Listen to this story about a poor young man and his great achievement, but don't focus on the details. Instead, let my words ring into your ear, each of them bringing you a step closer to a sound sleep.

He had never thought that he would be standing where he was that day in late October. With a poor upbringing and a mother who had worked long hours to pay rent and put food on the table, as a kid, Jason always assumed that he was destined for a similar life. After all, wasn't that what they always said – that the apple couldn't fall that far from its tree? And how could he had thought any different? Really, how could he, when his mother had to scrape the bottom to give him enough for school books and clothes. And even though schooling his only son was always her priority and motivation that got her through life – no one really thought that Jason could actually amount to much.

When his mother got sick, he was only 15 years old. While his friends were having fun and exploring life, he was the one worrying about food, bills, and being able to afford medicine for his sick mother. He never knew his father, for he had left them when Jason was just two years old, so he didn't have a single memory of the old man. It had always been just him and his mother against the world. And what a cruel world that was.

There were days when he would go to bed hungry, unable to fall to sleep due to his gut rumbling. There were days when he would put tons of layers of clothing just because he had outgrown his jacket and couldn't afford a new one. When it was raining, he would always come home with wet feet and soaked socks, because he had holes in his shoe soles. But it didn't matter. As long as he could afford enough for food, rent, and his mother's therapy, nothing else really mattered.

Jason used to spend his mornings in high school and his afternoons on whatever construction site would give him work. The nights were reserved for studying and 4-5 hours of sleep so he could endure the following day. Sometimes, he even took naps in the school's toilet between classes. It wasn't how a high school student should be spending his days, but he had no other option. Her mother took care of him for 15 long years – it was now his turn to earn. He was still a kid so he couldn't possibly ensure a good life for his mother, but at least with the money that he was earning for medicine, he could keep her alive.

At first, it seemed that help was coming from all sides – distant family, neighbors, colleagues of his mother – they all seemed to want to help. And they all did for a while. Sometimes the help was in form of old hand-me-downs, clothes from the children of his mother's friends that were a couple of years older than him. Sometime he would receive bags of groceries. Sometimes, although this happened rarely, he would get a check. But you can rely on such help for only a certain amount of time – after all, they had no close family to care for them. So, eventually, the whole weight of the burden was on his back, and he, even though a kid, was the only one who could wear it. His mother was too weak to walk, let alone work. There were days when she couldn't even get out of bed. So there was never a choice – he didn't choose to go to work or spend his days as single parents do – making ends meet and struggling – he simply had to find a way to earn if he wanted for him and his mother to stay alive.

But despite all of that struggle, he never gave up on learning. His mother used to always say to him that his books were his ticket out of misery. Only knowledge could save him. And even though he never really imagined that his books would get him somewhere in life, he obeyed his mother and studied hard. Maybe it was because there was a spark of belief inside of him that hoped that years from that moment, he could actually be living his life differently. Maybe it was just because deep down he knew that his mother would let go soon, so he saw this as his final gift to her.

When she passed away, after five years of battling the disease, she was already with a scholarship. At least she had lived long enough to see him getting somewhere. At one point, she actually said that to him – "I cannot express how deeply sorry I am that you had to endure the things you went through as a kid – no child should spend their innocent years that way – but in a way, I am glad that all that struggle had turned you into a truly honorable and good human being. You are very humble, I only wish you stay the same even after you earn millions. Because I know you will, I see the potential in you. You are one-of-a-kind Jason, so please, never change. Now that I have seen that you've paved the right road for your future, I can finally die in peace". And she did. She finally closed her eyes for good a week later.

Fifteen years after that moment, overlooking the city lights from his penthouse apartment, Jason remembered how he felt that day. So sad to listen to his mother talking about dying, but glad that he managed to make her proud, even after a tough childhood. Even though he had always doubted himself and thought that he would forever remain that little high school boy – working for scrapes and always tired – his mother's wish did come true, and he had reached greatness. Being a proud owner of a successful company and a giant in its category, Jason thanked his lucky star that night.

But he never forgot his mother's pleading. To stay humble and always be his true self. Now that he was worth millions, he still remembered that moment perfectly clear. He also remembered what got him to the top, as well. Hard work and steel motivation. It was a speech he gladly gave to his young and new employees, inspiring to be bold and take chances, always looking outside of the box, not settling for convenience. He used to tell him how he had spent his school days hungry and cold, but he kept on moving. "Because life doesn't stop just because you are tired or afraid. It keeps on going, new day rises, new opportunities open up" he used to say. "You could never know what door can suddenly open for you, so never give up".

Jason was also active in charity work. He had a foundation that primarily helped young kids from poor families achieve their dreams. In forms of scholarships, checks, and employment opportunities, he did not forget about such communities. He never forgot where he was coming from, which is probably why, he was sitting here today. Looking from the top, satisfied with his life.

He also had a family of his own now, so teaching the right lessons to his children was the most important thing he, as a parent could do. He gladly remembered his mother, how he always seemed to find a way to wear a smile on her face after two long shifts and a very thin stew. Even though they had to struggle to stay alive, she would always tell him to be strong, fight the things that cause you pain and discomfort, and find the opportunity in the books. He knew that, no matter how much money he had, he would let his kids find their own way, unspoiled and free to make their own choices. He would be there to help their dreams come true if needed, but he knew, even now, that he would do his best to instill work ethics and modesty.

Because in his mind, that was what made great people great – their ability to stay humble and know true values despite their endless opportunities that their money could buy them. Pursuing your dreams should not be about being better than others – it should be about working hard to be the best person you could possibly be.

The Golden Piano

Duration: 45 minutes

All of us have fond memories from our childhood – some things that bring back the same emotions that we used to experience when we were little. This story is about a woman about to re-discover feelings with the same depth as she did when she was a kid. So lie down comfortably in your bed, close your eyes, and let the words of this bedtime story put you in a relaxing mood, pushing you into a sound sleep.

Anna was ten years old when they sold their house by the lake and moved to the big city. As a little girl, she was sad to leave her friends and change school, but she was also very excited. Every movie she had ever watched was shot in the city. The streets were always crowded with people; there were chatter and music on every corner. Not unlike her underpopulated little town, sitting quietly by the river, never having exciting things to offer to its young residents.

Even though she had been living in her downtown apartment for more than two-thirds of her life, she always gladly remembered her first home. The place where she was born. The little white house with picket fence all around it. The home where she made her first steps, learned her first words, started school from… She remembered how she used to spend her afternoons there, sitting by the lake, feeding the ducks, hummin tunes silently not wanting to be heard. She had always been shy. Their parents had thought that she would overgrow the shiness over the years, but that never happened. Some things you are just bored with – she had to come to terms with the fact that she could faint anytime she was in front of a group of people.

You would think that such a person would choose a career as something that didn't involve too many people. Perhaps she could decide to be a writer, sitting quietly in her creative oasis, letting her imagination run wild on paper just because she couldn't express the same enthusiasm in real life. But no, despite the fact that she had always been a shy little girl, she chose to be a pianist – performing in front of large crowds, making thousands of people happy with her music. And it all started back in hr little hometown.

Back in the town by the lake, in the house next to theirs, there was an old woman living alone. The woman was an Auschwitz survivor, a true hero, and someone that Anna couldn't wait to spend time with. Every day after school, Anna would go there. The old lady would bake cookies that they used to devour with herbal tea, gladly. Anna was truly mesmerized with the lady. She loved listening to stories of war, the past, and what life had been like when the lady was young. But that was not the only thing that made Anna fall in love with the lady and her home. It was something else, actually.

In the sitting room, by the window overlooking the lake, there was a piano like no other. It was the most beautiful thing Anna had ever seen. It was wooden, but when the sunlight hit its surface, you could easily be tricked that it was mad entirely out of gold. Bright and shiny, Anna loved this golden piano.

Every day, after the talk was over, and just before it was time for Anna to go home, the lady would play a tune on the piano. Watching her play was almost otherworldly. Giving all of her self while playing, the lady showed Anna raw beauty that she hadn't thought existed. It was beauty and sadness tangled up together, wrapped in such strong emotions that seemed to come out of the lady's pores only when she was by the piano. Anna used to think about that. About these emotions. How they were bubbling up inside the lady until her fingertips touched the keys. Then they were unleashed. Let go to run wild over the keyboard, allowing the listener a peek into her soul.

Her first love for the piano came not from hers, but from the neighbor's house by the lake. Listening to the notes the lady hit, Anna knew that playing piano was what she was supposed to do.

When she was ten years old, her father's work got transferred to the big city, and they had to move. She was said to leave the lady because she knew that she would never listen to her play the golden piano again. She knew that she could never watch the sun rays illuminate her beautiful age-worn face while she was playing like an angel on this golden instrument. She was said about that, surely, but happy that she would have an opportunity actually to go to music school there and pursue her dreams. And that is precisely what Anna did.

Learning to play the piano was never hard for Anna – she was a natural at it. But she did have to work hard to stand out from the crowd, as there were many talented pianists in her school. But her hard work paid off when she got a scholarship and became one of the most respected pianists of her time.

But all these times, after every concert, every show, the picture of the old lady playing on the golden piano would come back to her vividly. She never knew what had happened to the lady or how she had spent her life – naturally, Anna assumed that she was no longer alive as she would be more than 95 years old. "What if she is alive?" Anna thought after one of her shows. "Would she even remember me?". The thought stayed in her mind for a couple of days, and so Anna finally got the courage to make a few phone calls and find out for herself.

After an hour or so, she learned the truth. The lady had passed six years ago in her sleep. Anna was glad that she had left the world so peacefully. She imagined it was also with grace, as that is what the lady had been her whole life – elegant and graceful. But that was not the only thing she found out. Apparently, she was buried in her backyard as the lady's wish had been not to leave the house. Her soul had left this world, but her body remained in her home. That thought made Anna smile with content, as that was so like the old lady. She had always been a fierce spirit. She could almost imagine arguing with her son, refusing to leave the house or to be buried elsewhere.

The old lady had a son that lived about 500 miles away, so he couldn't visit that often. However, he always used to make the time to check on his ma at least once a month. Anna remembered about the visits that he and his children had paid the old lady. After all, those were the times that the lady was truly happy.

With that on her mind, Anna spent the rest of the day thinking about the past and her childhood. Most of it all, thinking about the house of the old lady and her golden piano. She wondered whatever had happened to it. She couldn't shake the thought off, so she grabbed her laptop and started researching. She was looking for a way to contact his son. After just 5 minutes, she had his number. She was surprised to see that, even though he was 20 years older, he still looked just as she remembered him.

He picked up his phone after the very first ring. She didn't know why, but when she heard his voice, she felt butterflies in her tummy. Such a strange feeling that was. But that was not the strangest part. She was even more surprised that he remembered who she was. The man was almost 70 years old, but his memory was as sharp as ever. "Oh my god, Anna, I am so glad to hear from you. How have you been?" he asked her. She explained to him that she is a pianist, which he already knew, and then she went on talking about his mother, what big of an influence she had been on her and how it was her that had inspired Anna to pursue her dreams. Then she told him she had only found out about her death today. "You know, she used to mention you from time to time. I even think she used to keep tabs on you. I remember that she was proud when you had your first show, about 10-11 years ago, I guess" the man said. She couldn't believe it. "But why didn't she ever contact me? I feel almost ashamed for not doing the same thing, but I was just a kid when we moved here. I always thought she had long forgotten bout the little girl next door".

A tear met her cheek as she was listening to him talking about her life, and how he had to fly there more frequently because the lady was too stubborn to move to his place. So typical of her, she thought.

After a moment of silence, she finally bit the bullet and asked the question. "You know, the reason, well, one of the reasons why I called you is because I am curious about her piano. I understand that it has sentimental value to you, so please, don't be offended by my question, as it is definitely not my intention, but I wanted to know whatever happened to it. And if you still have it, would you be willing to sell it?" There, she said it.

After a sigh, the man said, "The piano is still in her house. I have no use of it, really. Yes, it has sentimental value as it was her most precious belonging, but neither me nor my kids play it. None of us was ever attracted to the music; I guess we inherited the wrong genes," he laughed. "It remained unmoved, even after a couple of decades. It is just where you remember it – next to the window overlooking the lake. I was actually planning to transfer it to storage these days as the house is for sale. I have viewers come and go all the time; I just don't feel comfortable with it sitting there, and I surely don't want to pass it on to some strangers."

Without even thinking, Anna asked if they could meet. They agreed to meet at noon the following day, so she had no time to waste. She knew what she had to do. She packed a small bag, booked a flight, and headed out.

The next morning, when she left her hotel room to go and meet with the man, she couldn't really believe what she was doing. Was this a good decision? Or was it something she decided in the spur of a moment based on her nostalgic feelings?

When they finally met, she explained to him why she had come. She wanted to buy the house, along with the piano. She would move the fence so that her grave could be on its separate plot so that his children could visit whenever they felt like it. Also, she promised that her door would always be open for his children and grandchildren if they ever wish to play the piano.

The man didn't even hesitate. He hugged Anna so tightly, she could barely let out a breath. "She would have wanted you to have it" he said.

A week later, when she finally got the keys, she headed there. She hadn't visited her hometown in over 20 years. You would think that buying a house would make her at least check the condition of it, but she believed the man and the photos she had shown her. When she finally got there, the place looked even more magnificent than she remembered. Although a bit dusty and in desperate need of some air, everything was in pristine condition.

Dust flew all around her when she finally pulled the sheets that were covering the golden piano. It was a sunny day, so when the sunlight hit the wooden surface, strong emotions hit her even harder. She couldn't help herself. She started playing a well-known melody that the old lady used to play to her and started crying. She couldn't believe how happy she felt.

She sighed with content, opened the door, and headed out to visit the lake. When she got out the door, she glanced at the house she knew too well. Although it had a different shade of color and a new fence, it was somehow the same. A woman that was staring out the window, gave her a wave. She waved back. She would introduce herself the following day. Today was reserved for paying tribute to the old lady. The lady who inspired her to believe in herself and follow her dreams. The lady that was to blame for her deep love for the piano. The old lady that she would always remember.

Chasing the Rainbow

Duration: 45 minutes

Revisiting places from our childhood that made us feel safe and secure when we were kids can spark the most intense feelings deep within us. This story is about something similar to that. It is a story about a man patiently waiting to recreate a childhood memory for the sake of making a loved one happy. It is calm and peaceful, so let my words put you in a relaxed mood. Close your eyes, and allow this story to help you fall asleep.

We all have a fond memory from our past. Something that puts a smile on our face every time we think of it. Perhaps a memory from our early childhood – the time when we were innocent and when the world was a better place. Sometimes, we are able to capture those memories in the form of photographs – a visual reminder of the time when we felt good. We keep those photos framed and displayed so that a mere look at them can ignite strong emotions and remind us that life can be good.

That was the case for Clint and his dad. For they have created such memory that stood framed in their living room – a souvenir of a good time. When he was just five years old, their family went on a camping vacation by the lake. It didn't look anything like the campsites today, but still, the concept was just about the same. You would park your RV or rent some of those ragged bungalows for a low price, and you can have a blast. Of course, that included a campfire, marshmallows, and food that otherwise is limited for indulgence at home. Clint loved that about vacations. It was the only time his mother wasn't too restrictive, so he could eat as much candy as he wanted and stay outside all day long, playing.

The campsite was in the woods, near the lake. He was only five years olf at that time, but even as a little kid he could detect real beauty. And this was simply magnificent. It was summertime, but it seemed as though the woods were following a different calendar. As the temperature there was barely warm. T-shirts at day were okay, but when night would creep in, you had to put on a sweater if you didn't want to catch a cold. And for his father, that was what a perfect vacation was supposed to be like. He absolutely hated the hot weather. You'd think he'd be used to it as they lived near the coast, but no. When June would roll in, he would automatically enter a three-to-four-month irritation mode. He used to sweat a lot, so whenever his forehead got shiny, you'd better steer clear from him, as his mood was about to get cranky. So this was just perfect. No sweat dripping, no wet shirts.

Thinking about that vacation now, Clint asked himself whether that was the reason for having such good memories of that summer in the woods. Because of his father's surprisingly good summer mood. He laughed at the thought as he was holding the frame and staring at the well-known photo. Of course, this was a copy he had made when he got married and moved to a new house. The original photo was still displayed proudly in his parents' house. It was his father's favorite photo, not only because he was holding his five-year-old son there, but also about the stong emotion that was bubbling up inside of him as his wife took the shot. He was happy, and that content was written all over his face that day. But that was not all. There was something about the light and the senery. And of course, the giant rainbow that spread up in the sky – in this photo over their heads.

Looking at the photo now, Clint could see the artistic side of it. Unfortunately, he had not inherited his mother genes – she was a painter and a master of anything art-related. He was a doctor and worked with facts. Science and theories that could be backed up. But looking at this now, he could notice that it wasn't just about the rainbow or their happy faces. It was about the angle, about the reflecting light… His mother was a real genius when it came to taking photos – and this one was one of her best works.

His father was turning 70 in a couple of weeks, which was a huge deal. He had finally retired and had come in terms with the fact that he got old. The 7 before the 0 was a clear sign. Clint used to joke with his father about his age on a regular basis; it was one of the things that lightened the mood during tense times. So, he wanted to do something special for the big day. He could buy him an expensive gift, but he knew his father – that wouldn't satisfy him. He would fake it, of course, and make a huge deal of it just so that Clint would think he had really nailed it, but in reality, he had never cared for the material stuff. So, what could you give a person like that? Something meaningful that would have deep sentimental value.

The other day, when Clint was going through the old photos and spotted this picture, it really hit him. That was the perfect gift for his 70-year-old dad, His son, Jamie, was just about to turn 5 in just a month and a half, about the same age as Clint when the photo was taken. And being such a deeply cherished memory, he came with the brilliant idea of him and his son recreating the same photo.

He immediately planned the trip for the three of them – himself, his wife, and their son Jamie. They booked their flight, and made a reservation for one spacious bungalow that was on that camping site. So basically, this was a two-in-one deal., A vacation for them, and a gift for his father. But that wasn't all – the trip would also enable Clint to bond with Jamie and create a memory that, hopefully, his son would also cherish after many years.

When they arrived at the site, the first thing that Clint noticed was how different the place looked. Almost unrecognizable, really. If it wasn't for the lake and the woods, he would think that he was visiting this campsite for the very first time. The truth? This had to be his sixth or seventh time, as they had spent many other summers there. But the view was one-of-a-kind. You couldn't forget it – not in a million years.

They headed for the reception to check-in, and Clint was surprised as to how quickly and smoothly the process went. He remembered how, when he was a kid, his father hat a couple of sheets of paper to fill in upon arrival. Today, everything was done electronically – the perks of digitalization and modern living. They grabbed their keys and entered their bungalow.

The bungalows were also nothing like Clint remembered – they were clean and sleek, and pretty well-equipped. To his surprise, their accommodation could also turn out to be up to high standards. And he was very glad since it had been over two years since their last vacation.

Once they had settled, Clint started studying the weather prognosis. They would only stay here for a few days, so he had to pinpoint the perfect time for them to climb the hill and take the photo. Because the photo was taken on the day when he and his parents decided to explore the woods. The day they got surprised by a quick and sudden rain that resulted in rainbows. He had climbed all the way up the hill, from where you could see the whole lake, the camping side, and the other part of the woods, as well. If he remembered correctly, it could take about an hour of hiking to get there. Therefore, he had to pick the time wisely. They couldn't possibly climb the hill twice – not with a needy toddler, at least.

Although these woods were known to be prone to rain and sudden changes in weather, how big were the chances of catching a rainbow there, really? But the rainbow itself wasn't that important. The photo would be just as good without it in it. After all, it is the thought, the effort, and the people in the photo that mattered. No matter what the weather or light would be like, he knew that his father would be thrilled with the gift.

And yet still, wouldn't it be great if they could actually catch a rainbow? So he should plan wisely. The best strategy was to climb there just before the rain would start, wait for it to be over, and take the photo as soon as the sun illuminates again.

So, that's what they did. The following they, they had packed a bunch of sandwiches, water, and snacks and headed up the hill. Although Clint had estimated that it would take them an hour to get there, they had already been hiking for 90 minutes, and they had still not reached the top. Perhaps he was not right about that. Or perhaps it was because they had to stop a dozen times on their way because of their not-so-fit condition. Whatever the reason, it didn't matter. The point was that they did manage to get to the top.

And, oh, it was so worth it. They could see the lake, their bungalow, and even the road in the great distance was partly visible. Tall pine trees were spreaded like a fence all across the lake as if they were hugging it, keeping it safe from harm. Jamie got a little bit scare of the height, but once Clint lifted him up, it seemed that all worries managed to disappear. He was so proud of being able to comfort his boy in times of need. He only hoped that things would be the same even after years passed.

Conveniently, as if the clouds were waiting for them to finally climb up, it started raining. There was a hole in the mountain nearby – almost like a cave, so they took shelter there. Jamie was more impressed with this cave-like thing than with the extraordinary view in front of him, but that was understandable since he wasn't even five years old, yet.

They ate a sandwich and waited for half an hour there, when the sun started peeking from behind the cloud. The rain wasn't giving up just yet, and yet it seemed like the sun was winning this battle. That put a smile on Clint's face as he knew – whenever rain and sun join their forces, rainbows appear. And almost magically, a colorful u-shaped rainbow appeared in front of them.

Clint took out the picture to make sure that the spot was exactly the same as the one in the photo. Then, he removed his and Jamie's raincoats, took him in his arms, and stood there, smiling, and waiting for his wife to take the photo. She took at least 20 photos with the rainbow in the background, so they could pick the winner later. Surprisingly, they were all great, so they had a hard time pinpointing which one to frame. Eventually, they agreed on one and headed down.

Now, Clint and his family were standing in front of his childhood home, ready to celebrate the 70th birthday of his father. He greeted them with a smile, and they walked in. It was a small celebration as his father was not the most socially-involved person. But it was perfect. Family and close friends were all they needed.

Little Jamie gave his grandpapa the gift. He started unwrapping, and Clint couldn't take his eyes off of him. He didn't want to witness the reaction. Suddenly, he jumped from his seat and grabbed his phone. He turned on his camera and waited. When his father was almost over with the unwrapping – it took him a while – he starting taking snaps.

The reaction was everything he could have hoped for and more. Pure joy was oozing from his pored. The happiness could be detected from miles away, which made Clint's heart melt. His father gave him a hug and thanked him for the most meaningful gift he had ever received. Without saying a word, he stood up and took the framed photo to the family room. He placed it next to the old one – the one with him and little Clint in it – and started crying.

Jamie ran toward his grandfather and gave him a smooch. He told him that he had spent the best time at the camping site, and that he would love to go there with his grandpapa someday, too. The grandfather looked at Clint with eyes that sparked happiness and mouthed a "thank you" that Clint would never be able to forget.

The Flight to London

Duration: 30 minutes

Lie down comfortably and close your eyes. Before we begin, make sure that you will have taken care of your bedtime routine and that you are ready to fall asleep. Good! Now, listen to this story carefully. Do not focus on the details - allow the words to float in your ears in a humming, and lulling way. Let this story help you fall asleep in under 30 minutes.

To Emily, airplanes had always been scary. There was something so frightening about how giant they were. They used to tell her that she would overcome this fear once she actually got into one, but that only added to her anxiety. How could something that huge fly? Oh, and the sheer thought of it being lifted from the ground. The thought of it flying so, so high up in the sky just gave her the chills. It was true! Emily was absolutely, utterly terrified of flying.

And yet, today, she was sitting in one. The seatbelt was on; everything as instructed. And still, she was so scared she thought she could die. It would take over seven hours for her to get from New York to London, and that was only making things worse. Seven long hours. Almost about the same time she spends in her office, working. Now, she is forced to spend that same amount of time flying in the sky.

But what other option was there really? She had done some research and found out that one can indeed take a charter boat from New York to London, but that would take her 17 long days. And besides, who could guarantee that she wouldn't get seasick? Of course, even she knew that wasting 17 days on a boat just because you didn't want to fly is ludicrous. So here she was, sitting by the window, not daring to look out.

Of course that the thought of not going had crossed her mind. But how could she when her baby sister was getting married in two days in London? She would never forgive her. If she was being honest, she wouldn't be able to forgive herself either.

A deep breath in. Another breath out. Breathe in. Breathe out. Wasn't that what they did in the movies? How come this didn't help her? Her palms were starting to sweat; she was starting to get jumpy. "Fear of flying" was written all over her face.

The flight was scheduled for 8 PM, so she had to make a plan. Her tactic was to get only a couple of hours of sleep so that she would be super tired on the plane and pass out. She had been awake since 2 AM, so why didn't she feel the need to fall asleep?

The plane had taken off, and 30 minutes had passed. Still, her eyes were wide open as she had drunk a couple of double espressos. She was just about to go to the toilet just to have something to do, when the nice old lady next to her asked, "Excuse me for asking, dear, but are you afraid of flying?" "Absolutely terrified," answered Emily. Then the woman asked her why on earth didn't she take a sleeping pill to help her sleep through the flight. But when Emily explained to her that she is more afraid of sleeping pills than she is of the actual flight, the woman had only a "Poor thing" to say.

"That was helpful," Emily thought, and instinctively shifted her head in the opposite direction, which was where the window was, so that was clearly a mistake. She became even more nervous and actually had to speak out the "Breathe in – breathe out" words to help herself come down. The woman notices and held her hand.

"I'm actually up since 2 AM. I barely got two hours of sleep, hoping that I will pass out quicker, but clearly, that doesn't work" Emily said, now feeling guilty of thinking that the old lady was unhelpful when all she was doing was trying to make things better for her. "Perhaps you are thinking about it too much, that is your problem. Try to distract yourself with other things so you can forget that you are actually on a plane. That should do the trick and help you fall asleep" the lady said. "Things like what?" Emily asked curiously.

Then the old lady told her that whenever she couldn't fall asleep, she just thought of some random, insignificant things to lull herself to sleep. "For instance, how about you do some observing? There are many people sitting in front of you, so how about you stop thinking about the plane, and focus on what they're doing instead. Here, let me start," she said. "You see that guy in the sixth row, the one with the blue shirt; he is looking pretty handsome. But he also has a nervous look on his face. If you look at him long enough, you may notice him looking at a picture of a woman and silently mouthing some words. I bet he is going to London to meet some girl. And from how he is looking, I assume the girl is pretty important to him. He does not want to screw that up".

"Now, that was pretty specific," Emily thought, surprised that this might actually work. So, she thanked the old lady for the advice and tried to do as told.

The first thing she noticed was an older gentleman snoring loudly in the distance. He was clearly keeping the woman next to him from getting a shuteye, as she kept on pushing and kicking him to either wake him up or at least turn the volume down. At least for some time.

Then there was this young woman who was obviously thrilled to be on the flight as she was constantly smiling, looking out the window, taking photos on her phone. She wasn't older than 20 or 22 years old, so she was clearly going somewhere fun.

In front of her, sat a mother who was desperately trying to calm down her crying baby. Rocking, singing, none of that helped. Her other son, a toddler of maybe 3-4 years, was playing video games pretty passionately, not quite caring for what was going on around him. "At least she doesn't have to worry about getting him to sit still," Emily thought.

A man sitting opposite from the woman with the kids was searching for something in his bag. It took him a while to find it, but when he did, a big smile appeared on his face. It was a yellow bag of M&M's. He lifted his hand and started shaking the bag in the air to get the baby's attention. And surprisingly, he did. The baby went from screaming to laughing out loud in seconds. Then the man handed the baby the bag, and he started playing with it in the most satisfying way possible. The woman thanked the man. She could finally rest a bit, as she was clearly feeling sorry for annoying the passengers.

In front of them, there was an old couple. They had at least 85 years each, and they were clearly still mad for each other. Holding hands and exchanging looks that only partners who had shared decades together knew how, they melted the hearts of everyone on the plane.

Beside them there was a businessman, constantly reading on his phone and taking notes in a classy notebook with his expensive pen. She assumed he was on his way to London to strike an important deal, so it was important for him to get all of the facts straight.

The woman next to him was secretly eyeing him from time to time, and since he wasn't wearing a ring, Emily wrote a happy ending for the two of them – they would exchange phone numbers by the end of the night. Then, he would call her, they would go out on a date, will have three beautiful kids and will live happily ever after in their big house in the suburbs.

The woman in the purple dress was looking annoyed.

The older man in row two was clearly sad about something.

The woman next to him was reading a book.

"Wake up; we've landed," the older lady next to her said. It took Emily a while to process what was really going through. Where was she? How did she get there? But when she looked out of the window and saw the plane grounded, a rush of joy flooded her. "The trick really helped. I was just looking at all of these people, distracting myself, and I must have dozed off. Thank you so much for sharing your advice with me." Emily said. The woman smiled and nodded and then got up to get her bag. Emily did the same, and they all left the plane.

Was she still afraid of flying? Absolutely! But did she find something to ease the anxiety and make the flights more bearable? That she surely did!

Part II: Guided Meditations and Self-Hypnosis

Relax Yourself to Sleep

Duration: 30 minutes

Are you feeling restless? Are you unable to lie still, with your eyes closed? Do you believe your mind wanders on its own, not allowing you to fall asleep? Do you really think that you have no control over what's happening to your body or brain? But, of course, you do! And this self-hypnosis/relaxation meditation will prove you just that. Not to keep you tossing and turning any longer, let's start this technique together now, shall we?

There are a few requirements, though. The first one is that you wear comfortable clothes. Make sure that the material of your pajamas is comfortable on your body so that it doesn't irritate your skin.

The next one is for you to create the perfect sleeping environment. That means that you should turn off the light, turn off the electronics in your room, adjust the temperature so that it is neither hot nor cold, and make sure that there's enough oxygen. A stuffy room can only add to anxiety and disturbing thoughts, so make sure to open the window to air out your bedroom.

Finally, lie in your bed, settling into a comfortable position. This is very important for self-hypnosis and meditation, as your body must be feeling at ease for it to be able to let go of tension.

Now, close your eyes!

Let's take a deep breath together. Inhale very deeply, feeling your lungs expand to the point when it almost feels they will burst. Hold, one, two. Now, gently, start releasing the oxygen very slowly through your nose, noticing the lungs deflate. Does that feel relaxing? Let's try it one more time.

Take a deep breath through your nose, then hold it for a second, two, three. Slowly, start releasing the air out, focusing on that sensation. Focusing on how your lungs come down.

Again, breathe in. Breathe out.

Breathe in. Breathe out.

Inhale deeply, exhale slowly.

Now, I will count to ten. You will focus your attention on my voice, not thinking of anything in particular. Just listening to my voice, letting the words ring in your ears. Listening and breathing. As I count to ten, you will breathe slowly, concentrating on the numbers.

1, 2, 3, 4, 5, 6, 7, 8, 9, 10.

Do you feel how the tension has started to give up. Let's do this once again.

1, 2, 3, 4, 5, 6, 7, 8, 9, 10.

Good! You're doing an excellent job. You are surpassing your fears or strong emotions, concentrating on your will to succeed – in this case relax and fall asleep.

Again, just breathe. Be in this moment, breathe slowly, follow the numbers, and focus on your gentle breath.

1, 2, 3, 4, 5, 6, 7, 8, 9, 10.

Can you see it? It turns out that you are indeed capable of relaxing yourself. Your mind may still not be aware of it, but your body is already feeling relaxed. Lying still, your body has taken on comfortable sensations – reliving the muscles from the tension it has started softening up the stiff parts, letting go of the discomfort that your long and busy day has caused.

You are also not aware of this, but with every second that passes in this position, and every breathe that you take, you are releaxing even more. Falling deeper and deeper into a calm state. So let's keep going.

I will now count to 20; you focus yourself on the breathing, acknowledging the numbers, allowing my words to announce the seconds, keeping your attention on how you inhale and exhale.

1, 2, 3, 4, 5, 6, 7, 8, 9, 10, 11, 12, 13, 14, 15, 16, 17, 18, 19, 20.

Every second is leading to your calmness and equilibrium. Your mind is now slowly starting to let go of the thoughts that keep you up all night. Your body is sending your brain signals that it has already entered a lighter state. Loosening up the tension, it nudges the brain to join the composure as well.

You still may not be able to notice this, but your mind has already started to unwind. Don't stop now. Let's keep going.

Take a deep breath, and just like before, hold it for a second or two. Through your nose, exhale very slowly, feeling your chest deflate, focusing on that sensation.

Repeat this one more time. A deep inhale. Hold, one, two, three. Then release the breath slowly through your nose.

Focus on what's going on in your mind right now. At this point, you are probably concerned with relaxing and falling asleep. That is trying too hard – the more you think that you need to fall asleep, the harder it is to do so. It is almost like telling a toddler not to touch something – the urge of reaching for that object is just too strong to resist at that point. The same thing happens with your mind.

Remember that the key here is not to fall asleep as quickly as possible – but as naturally as you can. That means to allow yourself – mind and body – to find the pace that they are comfortable with.

And distraction is your best weapon. So, keep thinking about your breath.

Breathe in. Breathe out.

Breathe in. Breathe out.

Breathe in. Breathe out.

Breathe n. Breathe out.

I will not count to 20 once more. Meanwhile, keep breathing slowly and gently.

1, 2, 3, 4, 5, 6, 7, 8, 9, 10, 11, 12, 13, 14, 15, 16, 17, 18, 19, 20.

Breathe in. Breathe out.

Breathe in. Breathe out.

With each breath, it is easier for you to let go and just relax. You are closer to ditching your thoughts entirely and just giving in to deep serenity. Each time that you inhale and exhale slowly, you get one step away from your busy mind. Think of your thoughts as strands that have you all tangled up. The more you breathe, the easier is for you to untangle.

So take another deep breath. Hold. Release slowly.

A breathe in. 1, 2, 3. A breath out.

Breathe in. Breathe out.

Breathe in. Breathe out.

To fall asleep, you have to stop listening to your mind. Stop paying attention to the thoughts and emotions that keep you from stepping into a sound sleep. Because that state of deep relaxation is there, waiting for you. All you have to do is untangle.

Follow my voice and just breathe. Imagine yourself detaching completely you're your thoughts and emotions. With each new number, each second that passes, you are untangling yourself, strand by strand, thought by thought.

1, 2, 3, 4, 5, 6, 7, 8, 9, 10, 11, 12, 13, 14, 15, 16, 17, 18, 19, 20.

You can almost feel it now. The trance is there. You are so close to entering the equilibrium that you can almost feel it loosening you up completely, making you feel heavier as though you are sinking into your bed.

Keep on sinking. Deeper and deeper. Feel your body loosening up, your mind unwinding. Keep breathing, and allow yourself to go deeper.

Breathe in. Breathe out.

You are still sinking.

Breathe in. Breathe out.

Deeper and deeper.

Breathe in. Breathe out.

You are feeling as though you are falling into a pit. You cannot see the bottom, but you are not feeling afraid. On the contrary, falling feels good at this point. Falling is something that you want to be doing. It relaxes you. It makes you feel lighter. It brings you closer and closer to the state of deep relaxation. You are almost there. Just keep falling.

Breathe in. Breathe out.

Breathe in. Breathe out.

You are still falling.

Breathe in. Breathe out.

It almost feels like floating at this point. You have slowed the pace, and you are just enjoying your fall now. Getting down slowly, light as a feather, you can feel your whole being relaxing. Resting in bed, away from you thoughts and free of emotions, you feel as though you can almost reach the trance.

Almost there, keep breathing.

A deep breath in. A slow breath out.

Breathe in deeply. Breathe out slowly.

Now, I will count to 30. Just stay focused on your breath. Focused on how you are slowly falling down, feeling more and more relaxed. With every breath, and every second that passes, you are getting sleepier and sleepier. Your eyes are getting heavy, and you are getting ready to let go. To step into deep equilibrium.

1, 2, 3, 4, 5, 6, 7, 8, 9, 10, 11, 12, 13, 14, 15, 16, 17, 18, 19, 20, 21, 22, 23, 24, 25, 26, 27, 28, 29, 30.

Breathe in. Breathe out.

Breathe in. Breathe out.

You are entering the trance. Allow this state to consume you all. Absorbing all of your feelings and emotions, you give in. You are relaxed. Sleepy.

Getting sleepier.

And sleepier.

Breathe in. Breathe out.

Breathe in. Breathe out.

Sleep…

Barefoot in the Park – Guided Relaxing Meditation to Help You Fall Asleep

Duration: 30 minutes

Visualization can be a powerful tool for knocking down the piled up tension from your mind, as well as from your body. By visualizing things that make you feel safe and relaxed, it is easier for you to rest and allow yourself to drift off. You can experience different sensations and enter a calm state that will help you fall asleep easier.

This guided meditation will help you do just that. We will take a barefoot walk in the park, and through the feelings and emotions that you can experience in such an environment, we will try to relax your whole being. By doing so, you can fall into a sound sleep in less than thirty minutes.

So let's begin. First, make sure that you have found a comfortable sleeping position. Tossing and turning at this point will only make you feel more anxious, and it will also be counterproductive. So, make sure that you are comfortable and that you will not be distracted.

For this to work, your eyes need to be closed.

Let's start by focusing on the breath. This is how most meditations start, mainly because calm breathing is a great way to detach yourself from your surroundings, which helps relax.

So, in goes a deep breath. Notice how your chest puffs up when you are inhaling. Now, release the breath through your nose, and see how the chest comes down at this point.

Repeat this again. Breathe in deeply. Breathe out.

Breathe in – puff up. Breath out – deflate.

Breathe in. Breathe out.

A breath in. A breath out.

Keep breathing deeply and calmly. Breathe out slowly.

1, 2, 3, 4, 5, 6, 7, 8, 9, 10.

Have you entered your sleeping mode? Good! Then we can proceed.

Take another deep breath. Then breathe out slowly. Continue breathing calmly, only this time, shift your attention to my voice, instead. Do not focus on your chest nor how deep breathing makes you feel. Instead, keep on breathing, but concentrate on the words, and try to visualize the scenario.

Imagine yourself standing in your favorite park. The weather is perfect for picnics and long walks. The sun is warm, but there is also a slight breeze that cools it off almost instantly, leaving a pleasant touch on your skin.

You must have visited this part of the park hundreds of times before, but you have never felt this liberated before. That's because there is no one around. No people, no dogs, even the squirrels have managed to stay away. It is just you and the lush green grass underneath your feet.

Try to visualize this scenario while breathing calmly. You are in a park, all alone. The weather is just ideal for outdoor activities The grass is green and thick, so you decide to take off your shoes.

It is morning, so the grass is still moist from the dew. Before you start walking, you decide to spend a few minutes just touching and treading the grass with your feet. Concentrating on how it connects with your skin, focusing on the sensations it leaves.

Now, you take your first step, barefoot, and you feel the coolness that moist grass leaves on your skin. You keep on going, experiencing the dampness on your feet. You relate to the energy of the earth in a way that is new to you. You have never been this connected to nature before. It is a mere act of walking, and yet, it feels extremely regenerating.

Now, take a deep breath again, and try to really imagine yourself walking down a field covered with lush grass. Keep on breathing and walking, trying to really feel the tingling on your feet that barefoot walking. I will now count to 20, and you will continue walking barefoot. Stay in the park, visualize this practice.

1, 2, 3, 4, 5, 6, 7, 8, 9, 10, 11, 12, 13, 14, 15, 16, 17, 18, 19, 20.

Continue walking, thinking about how uplifting this activity actually is. There is an exchange of energy between you and the earth going on. You absorb all of the positivity about it, letting it drain your thoughts and negative feelings. You begin to feel your senses rejuvenate. Your mind calms down.

But it is not your mind and emotional side that gets relaxed. Walking barefoot, you begin to notice that your feet are engaged in a very different way now. Their muscles support a walking pattern that is more natural to us humans – something that no shoes could replicate. You feel your ligaments stretch, your whole legs relax. You can feel your whole posture becoming more natural, all pains and aches disappear.

Try not only to visualize this scenario, but do your best to experience it as well. As you keep breathing, imagine your legs relaxing, your whole body becoming more and more comfortable. There is no more tension.

Keep on walking and feel the sun and breeze dancing on your skin. You keep walking, feeling the thickness of the moist grass on your feet, enjoying the cool and damp touch. All of the benches are empty – you are the only person there, but you don't feel like taking a break there. You want to further connect to nature, so you take a seat under a large tree.

From there, you can see the most of the park. With no one around, the sight almost seems surreal. Take a deep breath and try to imagine such a lovely landscape. Breathe out slowly, concentrating on the chirping of the birds.

Breathe in, absorbing all of the greenness and liveliness of the grass, trees, flowers, and nature around you.

Breathe out, focusing on the sound of the birds, as though you are contributing to the chirping.

Breathe in - let the green sight calm you down.

Breathe out – allow the lovely melody that the birds make to relax you.

Breathe in. Breathe out.

Breathe in. Breathe out.

Breathe in. Breathe out.

As I count to 10, focus on the overall sensations that would take over you in such a scenario.

1, 2, 3, 4, 5, 6, 7, 8, 9, 10.

Do you feel calmer already?

Now, imagine yourself getting up and starting to walk again. Re-discover the tingling sensation and coolness on your feet again, but do not place all of your attention there. You keep walking, but as liberating as that feels, you are also beginning to discover a new sensation – sleepiness.

Your muscles are steel loosened up and relaxed, but you are starting to notice that walking becomes heavier, harder. But you keep on walking because you haven't reached your final destination.

You take another step, just as heavy as the last one, and another, and yet another. Your arms are also becoming heavier, and you feel that your eyes are half-closed already. There is a rush of tiredness flooding you, and you feel like all you can do now is just lie down and sleep. But you are not there yet. So keep on walking.

Take another deep breath and feel your whole body getting heavier. Breathe out.

You don't have to imagine the heaviness of your body parts now, because it is really happening. You feel as though the bed has absorbed at least half of you – the other half still fighting to stay awake. Try not to fight it – give in.

Take another breath. Breathe out.

Breathe in. Breathe out.

A deep breath in. A slow breath out.

Inhale. And exhale.

Inhale. Exhale.

Let's return to the park. You are still walking. Still barefoot. Still moist underneath your feet. The cool touch is still there. But it's not as refreshing anymore. In fact, you feel like you need to throw something over your body, as the breeze is clearly winning the fight with the sun. Blowing stronger, becoming harsher.

But you keep on walking. And walking. Finally, you see two blankets. Imagine yourself spreading out one of the blankets over the grass. You lie on top of it and throw the other one over your body to keep you warm.

There is no one around. You are all alone. You are too tired to think this over. You just want to close your eyes and sleep.

Breathe in. Breathe out.

Breathe in. Breathe out.

Imagine yourself falling asleep under a tree. The chirping of the birds so lulling. The smell of fresh grass almost sedating.

Heavy and sleepy, you are ready to doze off. Return to your breath again, allowing each breath to bring you closer to a deep state of relaxation.

Breathe in. Breathe out.

Breathe in. Breathe out.

I will now count to 20, and you will keep on breathing, feeling yourself sinking in the bed, allowing a trance-like state to take over.

1, 2, 3, 4, 5, 6, 7, 8, 9, 10, 11, 12, 13, 14, 15, 16, 17, 18, 19, 20.

Ready to drift away.

So sleepy.

Sinking heavily.

Breathing calmly.

Slowly.

Getting more and more tired.

Give in…

… and sleep.

Training the Mind to Sleep with Self-Hypnosis

Duration: 45 minutes

This is a meditation that uses self-hypnosis as a technique to help you train your mind to sleep. Because that is indeed possible. You may think that you cannot fall asleep on cue or that you cannot do it without a pill, but unless you have a certain medical condition that requires sleeping aids, I guarantee that you can succeed.

We will take a few different steps that will lead us to the self-hypnosis – we will not do it outright because that will not work if you are feeling anxious. In order to find your anchor that you can later use for this purpose, you will first have to understand your mind, relax, let go of anxieties and negative feelings, and give in completely.

So, let's begin. For this to work, I highly suggest you do this practice only at night when lying in your bed, ready to fall asleep. So, wear comfortable clothes, settle into a good sleeping position, and close your eyes. Assuming that all of your electronic devices are off and that you have taken care of distractions, we can now proceed.

Let's start by thinking about your problem. What keeps you from falling asleep. That voice inside your head that has you tricked into thinking that you cannot fall asleep quickly - that you will spend the entire night tossing and turning, not being able to get a decent shuteye. That is precisely why you cannot. Because you believe so. The mind is a very powerful thing. Our beliefs are what guides us through. If you shift your mind into thinking that you can fall asleep, you will start to believe that. And that's when sleeping will come easily.

So let's think about that. Take a deep breath and hold it for a couple of seconds. Release slowly through your nose. Think about the process of sleeping. What sleeping actualy is. The act of closing your eyes and drifting off into a land of peacefulness. Think about how sleep is what you need after a long day. How your whole being craves this deep rest – to recharge, rejuvenate the senses. It is what you want. It is what you deserve.

Now, take another deep breath. Release slowly. And again. A deep breath in. A slow breath out. Keep on thinking about what sleeping is and what it does to your body.

Breathe in. Breathe out.

Breathe in. Breathe out.

Think about relaxing. About getting in bed, and stretching your legs, allowing your mattress to hold your whole body in such a comfortable way. Think about how your body gets heavier right before you are about to doze off. Think about that heaviness. Try to really feel it.

Start from your feet. Feel them get heavy. Tired, pulsing, glad they are finally getting some rest.

Go upward, through your ankles and calves, to your knees. They are heavy as well.

Feel your thighs, focus on how this part of your body feels. Gently move your attention up to your hips, feel the heaviness around your pelvic area.

Moving up to your belly, get to your chest. Take a deep breath and feel them puff up, Release the tension when breathing out slowly, feeling this body part deflate.

Keep on going upward, through your shoulder blades to your neck. How does this feel? Is it stiff? Or is it getting heavier and relaxed? Tilt your head a bit if needed to relax any tension.

Gently move to your head. Feel the heaviness of your cheeks, your eyes. Feel the tiredness that the long day has left on your face.

Now, just as gently, slide down back to your feet. Only this time, go through the back of your head, the back of your neck, your back…

When you finally reach your feet again, take a deep breath. Hold it for two seconds, then release slowly.

Breathe in. Breathe out.

Breathe in. Breathe out.

A breath in. A breath out.

Inhale. Exhale.

Breathe in. Breathe out.

Now, as you're slowly getting relaxed, think about sleep again. Only this time, try not to focus on what you think you know about it. Forget everything you've ever associated with sleep. Clearly, it didn't work. Sleep is not something that you can force yourself into. You cannot trick yourself into getting into this state. You can only prepare your body for this act. So, think of sleep as being something that your body will allow to happen. You cannot force it, you don't sneak up on it. It is something that occurs naturally when your senses allow.

You don't need to try too hard. All you need to do is to put your whole body into a state of relaxation. And that is exactly what we are doing.

Let's go back to your breath.

Take a deep breath through your nose. Hold for one, two, then release through your nose again, very slowly.

Again, breathe in deeply, breathe out slowly.

Breathe in. Breathe out.

I will now start counting, and you will stay focused on your breath, allowing my words just ring in your ears. Acknowledge the sound of the words, but stay focused on your breath. On the air that comes in and goes out of your body. And on your body, and how deep breathing makes you feel.

Now, Breathe in. Hold, one, two, breathe out.

1, 2, 3, 4, 5, breathe in.

7, 8, 9 breathe out.

11, 12, 13, 14, 15, keep on breathing.

17, 18, 19, 20.

Breathe in, 23, 24, 25.

Breathe out, 27, 28, 29, 30.

Can you feel the relaxation? It is almost there, within reach. It feels as though you can reach out your hand and grab this deep state of calmness. Surrounding yourself with the peacefulness, allowing your whole being to be in an utter equilibrium. Feeling your senses turn down, one by one, letting go of the reality and sinking into this new experience.

Now that your body and mind are relaxed, let's try to find your anchor. An anchor can be a cue word or even a physical sign that you will establish to associate you with the deep state of relaxation that you're just about to experience.

Once you get experienced in meditating before sleep, you can use your anchor to immediately transfer yourself to a state of relaxation, as that will become your sign to detach from everything and automatically put yourself in a calm mood.

To do that, you need to relax even deeper. So, let's keep on breathing.

Another deep breath in. Slowly release through your nose.

Do not think of anything in particular, just be in the moment, enjoying your breaths, one by one, each bringing you a step closer to a complete tranquility.

Breathe in. Hold the breath, one, two. Breathe out slowly through your nose.

Breathe in very deeply. Hold, one, two, three. Let go gently and slowly.

Inhale deeply. Hold the breath. Exhale slowly.

Breathe in. Hold, one, two. Breathe out.

Breathe in. Hold for two seconds. Breathe out.

Breathe in. Stop. Hold. Breathe out.

Breathe in. Breathe out.

Breathe in Breathe out.

Inhale deeply. Exhale slowly.

In through your nose. Out through your nose. Your breath is all there is right now.

Breathe in. Breathe out. You are falling deeper and deeper.

Breathe in. Breathe out. Getting heavier and heavier.

In again. Slowly out.

1, 2, 3, 4, 5, 6, 7, 8, 9, 10, 11, 12, 13, 14, 15, 16, 17, 18, 19, 20.

Breathe in. Breathe out.

If you think you need more time to relax more deeply, continue breathing for another minute or so. When you're ready, think about the anchor that you want to use. Your anchor can be anything. You can decide to say the cue word "relax now" or "deeper" or "let go." But it doesn't have to be a word. Your anchor can also be a physical sign. For an instant, you can choose to pinch your arm or bring together your pinky and thumb. Just choose what you want to be your anchor at this point. The important thing is for you to remember the anchor as you will use it on those nights when you feel the need for self-hypnosis.

Now, breathe again. Slowly and deeply.

I will count to 10 now, and you will use that time to get heavier. Use the time to sink deeper into your bad, feeling more and more relaxed.

Breathe in. Breathe out.

1, 2, 3, 4, 5, 6, 7, 8, 9, 10.

Can you feel yourself relaxing more deeply? Keep breathing and focus on how your body feels at the moment, Just as you are starting to feel like you are very heavily sinking deeper, set your anchor.

Now that your anchor is set, you've captured the state of relaxation that you wish to be in. You can later use this as a mental trigger, as a shortcut to peacefulness. By setting your anchor, you are adjusting your preferred state of mind, as you see fit – relaxed and free of anxieties and worries. When your anchor is set, you allow yourself to enter and stay in a calm place.

With a set anchor, you are starting to believe that sleep is indeed possible. You become aware of your relaxation, aware of the heaviness of your body, aware that you are now in a state that is neither reality neither a dream.

You are not asleep yet, but you are not fully awake either. You are now in a state of trance. Once you get into a trance, your body will let you know. There will be a slight movement of your thumb or another finger, perhaps. That is just your body signaling a different state. Don't fight it, don't try to force it, or even assist. Just lie still, with your eyes closed, deeper into calmness, allowing your body to do its thing.

It doesn't have to be a full movement. You can feel just a small tremor, and that will still announce that you've entered the trance.

So, I will now count to ten, allowing you to get used to this new state.

1, 2, 3, 4, 5, 6, 7, 8, 9, 10.

Now that you know that you are in a trance, allow your body and mind to get used to this new feeling. Notice how this state feels. Especially if this is your first time in trance, learn all about it now, so you can easily recognize it on other nights.

Feel what it really is like to be trapped in between two states – unconsciousness and awareness. Feel the peaceful alertness that you are experiencing at this moment.

Notice your body, how different it feels now.

Notice your breath. Breathe in. And breathe out. Pay attention to the air going in and out of your nostrils, and how even the mere sensation of breathing doesn't feel the same again.

Trance seems different. It is kind of a weird feeling, but in good way. Your body feels odd, but you somehow feel like staying in this moment forever. Not fully aware, not sleeping either.

There is no need to hurry, no need for rushing. If you are truly enjoying your trance, allow your body and mind to get properly introduced to it. You can stay in this state for as long as you like. All you have to do is to keep breathing calmly and enjoy the new sensations that have taken over your whole being.

I will now slowly count to 20, allowing you the time to enjoy the trance.

1, 2, 3, 4, 5, 6, 7, 8, 9, 10, 11, 12, 13, 14, 15, 16, 17, 18, 19, 20.

Think about this state and how easy was for you to get into it. You can do this every night if you want to. You can just set your anchor and feel yourself slide away into a completely different world. Somewhere between the dream and reality.

You may not be able to feel it at this point, but your body is getting more and more relaxed with every second that passes. It is easier for you to breathe in; it feels even lighter to breathe out. You have done this. You have managed to put yourself into this state. You can also all into a deep and sound sleep.

If you tune out this very second, you will probably be seconds away from dozing off. Because your body is so relaxed and your mind calm and free of thoughts, you are just moments away from falling asleep.

You are breathing slowly. In and out. Inhaling and exhaling. Feeling the breathing sensations in your nostrils… Filling up your lungs.

You are almost there. Keep going.

Just feel your whole being craving rest.

Breathing and feeling your body go so heavy, that it almost feels as though the bed has swallowed you. You are sinking deeper. And deeper. And deeper.

Sliding away.

Letting go of everything.

Just waiting for the unconsciousness to roll over. Allowing you to rest and rejuvenate.

Slowly. Calmly.

Feeling relaxed. Deeper and deeper.

Breathing in and out. In and out.

Letting go.

Feeling it taking over. Allowing sleep to take over.

Giving in…

Sleep…

Entering Sleep – Guided Meditation
Duration: 50 minutes

If you believe that sleep is something that can be seen, will you ever be able to find it? One of the main reasons why people stay up all night even when they are tired, is because they try too hard. You cannot force yourself to fall asleep. You need to open your senses and allow them to detach from the reality, one by one, slowly. You need to enable your body to relax completely and be able to enter a different state. You need to let your mind let go of thoughts and anxieties. You have to work with your whole being, and most importantly, listen to what it has to say. And this meditation will help you do just that.

Assuming that sleep is something that you can actually see and find, we will go on the ultimate hunt tonight. We will pass many obstacles, shut down many doors, allowing your body and mind to get to that deep relaxation, slowly and at their pace.

Now, let's begin. Start by lying in bed comfortably. Your eyes should be closed, and you need to make sure that there isn't anything that can interrupt this practice and drag you back to your conscious reality.

Once that's all taken care of, take a deep breath. Through your nose and deeply. Hold it for two seconds. Then release it slowly through your nose again.

Breathe in deeply. Hold, one, two. Breathe out.

Breathe in through your nose. Hold for two seconds. Exhale.

Breathe in. And breathe out. In and out. In and out.

I will now count to 10, and you will continue with the breathing, only this time, do not hold the breath in, just breathe in and out as calmly as possible, trying to put yourself in a more relaxing mood.

1, 2, 3, 4, 5, 6, 7, 8, 9, 10.

Now that we have slowly started to detach from our surroundings, we can start.

Picture yourself in a dark room. There is no one beside you in that room. No objects nearby, nothing. You are standing in the middle of this empty room, and yet, you are not alone. You can sense that there is something that's keeping you company. It is your thoughts, but they are not good thoughts. It is your fears, uncertainties, and anxieties that are surrounding you at this moment.

Your will to fall asleep quickly is also there. Keeping you further from relaxation, feeding your anxieties. You want to fall asleep, but you know that you cannot do it outright. Sleep just doesn't come naturally to you. How does that make you feel? Are you frustrated? Or maybe you're feeling angry with yourself? The more you think about it, the less likely you are to drift off. Which is a good thing at this moment, as we need to paint a very clear picture as to what happens when you think and not think about things.

Observe your thoughts and feelings for a moment. Feel their presence. Allow them to take over you for a minute. Now, try to picture them, leaving your mind and body, and physically surrounding you in that room. They are all around you. You can see them clearly. The room is getting stuffy, your breathing is getting heavier. You feel trapped, and you need to get away.

So you start pushing forward. It is hard and it takes a lot of strength, but you are doing it anyway. You have no other choice. If you stay with your thoughts and anxieties, you feel that you will suffocate. Imagine yourself pushing, trying to break free.

You see a door in front of you. It is close, and yet it seems so far away. But you keep on pushing. Harder and harder. You strengthen out your hand to see if you could reach the doorknob. You are almost there. Keep on pushing. Harder. Even harder. Your fingertips have already touched the doorknob, just a little bit closer. And closer. There! You open the door and push yourself out of the room. You shut it well, glad to have left all of your thoughts and feelings trapped inside. You have gotten away.

You exit the room, only to be found in a long and narrow hallway. There are no other doors in sight, the end of the hallway cannot be seen. You only have one option – to go straight ahead. So that's what you're doing – you start walking.

Try to really imagine yourself in this scenario, walking down this narrow path, with nothing in sight. Keep walking and walking. I will now count to 10, and you will continue walking.

1, 2, 3, 4, 5, 6, 7, 8, 9, 10.

You keep on going, and all of a sudden, you see a door to your right. You grab the doorknob with your hand, and you enter the room. Just like with the previous room, there is nothing here. No objects, nothing on the walls. You stand in the middle of this white room, but something is different – you don't feel the same anymore. A strange sensation is starting to take over you. A powerful feeling floods your senses. You are there, aware, but somehow you feel different. As if you are starting to get numb. And more numb. Your whole body is getting heavier. Try to feel this sensation.

Starting at your feet, feel a heavy-like sensation flowing upward. Feel the numbness in your ankles, then spreading to your calves, knees, thighs. Feel your legs getting heavier. Imagine yourself standing in the middle of this strange room, with your legs almost nailed to the floor.

But it's not just your legs that are heavy. You can feel the numbness throughout your whole body. Feel it in your hips, your abdominal area… Do not just imagine this. Try to really feel your body getting heavy, as you are lying in your bed, getting ready to fall asleep.

From your abdominal area, move up to your chest – feel the heaviness there. Take a deep breath and let it out slowly. Try to break the tension-like numbness that you feel in this part.

Move upward to your shoulders and neck. Focus on the numbness there for a second, then let it spread to your head. All across your face, forehead, that heavy sensation has spread throughout your whole body.

From your head, move it downward, back through the neck, shoulders, then through your upper arms, elbows, hands, fingers… Feel both of your arms taking on a numb-like sensation.

You are standing heavily, feeling as though you cannot lift your leg or even move a finger. But you know that you have to keep on moving. , and You need to find a way out.

There is another door that you have to open. Although it feels impossible, you somehow manage to make a move. You grab the doorknob, open the door, get out of the room, and then close the door shut behind you.

It is another hallway but very different than the last one. This one isn't as narrow, with a lot of natural light. Once you start walking, you also notice that there is a light breeze giving you a refreshing and cool feeling. You don't know where it is coming from, but it feels good.

Keep walking. Ahead. And ahead. Your body is still heavy, you still feel that numb sensation throughout. But you keep on walking. Feel the breeze in your hair, across your face, just dancing on your skin. Leaving a cool touch. Keep on walking and breathing.

Breathe in. Breathe out.

Breathe in. Breathe out.

As you are walking, you see that the hallway is getting lighter and lighter, but it is not just light, it is also warmth that has you feeling different. It is the sun that has lighted up the path and warmed up your skin. You don't see it, but you feel its presence. Focus on this feeling. How the sun and the breeze combined feel. Although you are feeling heavy, there is a very pleasant feeling taking over. You almost feel like walking in the park on a perfect spring day. Keep on walking.

Breathe in. Breathe out.

Breathe in. Breathe out.

You keep walking, but you realize that the hallway seems different – it is wider now. You keep on walking, and you notice how the walls are actually moving. They are moving wider apart, creating this huge space that is getting even bigger with every step you take, every second that passes.

The sun is still present; the breeze is also there to cool down the warmth. But there is another thing that is different now. There is no ceiling. Instead of the ceiling, there is an open space that allows you to see the sky now.

Clear and sunny, you enjoy the view. Imagine yourself walking down this path that has become a wide and open space now. When you look up, the blue sky is there to greet you, the sun to leave a warm and gentle touch on your face.

You keep on walking, but you are still feeling heavy. The walking has been tiring. Your muscles crave rest, but you are nowhere near done. You cannot stop now. You still haven't found what you have been searching for – the deep and relaxing sleep. So you keep on going.

The tiredness and heaviness make you want to sit down and take a rest, but a the same time, you are feeling strangely light and content. It is contradictory – to be feeling heavy and light at the same time, but that is precisely how you feel at this moment. Heavy physically, light mentally.

Take a deep breath, and keep on going. You are breathing calmly and walking slowly. There is no reason for you to be rushing now. You are in no hurry. In fact, the lightness you feel mentally – the fact that your mind is free of any thoughts, is so liberating that you don't want this to end. It feels good to be in your skin right now. It feels good to be walking under the sky.

Breathe in. Breathe out.

Breathe in. Breathe out.

You notice that the walls have gotten so wide apart, that you can barely even see them. Keep breathing and imagine them getting further and further away. I will now count to 10, and you will stay focused on your walking, breathing, imagining the walls disappearing from sight.

1, 2, 3, 4, 5, 6, 7, 8, 9, 10.

Now that the walls have become barely visible pots in the distance, the space is completely exposed. Open to the outside, you are no longer in a hallway. The narrow pathway that you were walking on earlier is now just a path in the middle of a lush meadow. There is nothing confining you, you can breathe freely, walk freely.

You are still feeling tired and heavy. Getting even heavier with every breath. Yet surprisingly, you feel as though you can be walking like this for hours.

Take your time to really absorb every detail that is surrounding you at this moment. There is the green in the grass – the thick, lush grass - calming your eyes. The colorful flowers that are providing a vibrant pop, making the meadow look even more magnificent.

The birds flying around. The buzzing of the bees. The butterflies that you see flying in every direction. The sun warming up your face, the breeze dragging a cooler touch.

You are walking down the pathway and breathing. Calmly and slowly. A breath in. A breath out.

Breathe in. Breathe out.

I will now count to 20, very slowly. Use that time to see yourself in such a scenario, walking at a slow pace, just breathing in the lovely nature around you.

1, 2, 3, 4, 5, 6, 7, 8, 9, 10, 11, 12, 13, 14, 15, 16, 17, 18, 19, 20.
Can't you feel how heavier your body has become? Your eyelids are starting to lower, you feel as though you are dragging your feet across the pathway. You breathe in. And out. In and out. You are feeling calm and more relaxed. Each breath is getting easier and lighter than the last one.

Let the chirping of the birds guide your way. Listen to that beautiful and lovely melody. Let it ring in your ears, providing comfort, lulling your senses.

Getting more tired and tired now.

You feel like you can give in at any moment now.

Almost there.

You keep on walking slowly, very slowly, in fact. You have decreased the pace to the point that you are barely even moving. But you are moving. You know that you haven't found what you came here to find.

So keep on breathing. Calm ad relaxed. Breathe in and breathe out.

A deep breath in. A slow breath out.

Inhale and exhale. Inhale and exhale.

All of a sudden, a door appears in front of you. You want to hurry toward it, open it in a hurry, see what's on the other side, but you can barely even move. You are so tired. So you take your time.

A breath in. A breath out.

Breathe in. Breathe out.

Finally, you reach the doorknob. You open the door wide, and enter a room.

It is a room but it looks exactly like the outside – the meadow, the sky, the birds, the flowers… they are all there. And yet, it is kind of secluded. It feels weird, almost dreamy. Maybe it is a dream. You are not quite sure anymore. All you know is how tired you are.

The minute you enter the room, the heaviness increases extremely. You put yourself in a lying position, and you close your eyes gently.

Allowing the birds to calm your whole being, turn down your senses, lull you to sleep.

Because you are sleepy.

So tired and heavy.

Your eyelids are pressing into your eyeballs.

Craving rest.

Wanting to rest.

Needing to sleep.

Calm and relaxed, ready to doze off.

Drift away into another dimension.

Sleep…

The Rainy Day – Stress Relief Guided Meditation

Duration: 30 minutes

Our days are packed with busy chores and tight schedules. After being involved in so many different activities, it seems hard to switch your mind off and allow yourself to relax. But it is possible. By setting only 30 minutes aside, this pre-sleep (or late afternoon) meditation will put you in a calm mood, detaching your mind from unimportant thoughts, keeping stress and anxiety at bay.

If you are practicing this to fall asleep, then lie on your bed, settled in a comfortable sleeping position. If you want just to relieve yourself from daily stress, then you can be seated. The important thing is for you to be comfortable. Ideally, your eyes should be closed. Keep your hands at your sides, and let's begin.

Let's start by drawing our attention to the breath. Take a deep, but very calm breath. Keep it in for two seconds. Release it slowly through your nose. Let's do this again. Breathe in calmly and deeply. Hold for two seconds. Breathe out through your nose, slowly. And again. Breathe in deeply. Hold, one, two. Breathe out.

Breathe in [pause]. Breathe out.

Breathe in [pause]. Breathe out.

Inhaling deeply [pause]. Exhaling very slowly.

Focus on the sensation that deep and calm breathing brings. Put your attention not only on the act of breathing but on the breath itself. Feel it entering your nostrils, flowing through them, filling your lungs, making your chest puff up. Now feel your lungs shrink, your chest deflate. Feel the air going out of your nostrils. Can you feel how calming this is?

Do it once more. Take a deep and calm breath. Hold for two seconds. Breathe out very slowly.

Breathe in [pause]. Breathe out.

I will not count to 10 very slowly, allowing you the time to just be in this moment. Be present, aware of your breath, noticing the sensation that deep breathing brings.

1, 2, 3, 4, 5, 6, 7, 8, 9, 10.

Do you feel calmer already? Can you notice the difference? Can you see what something as simple as breathing can mean for your whole being. Lifting up the mood, bringing peace to your spiritual self. Allowing the mental and physical to find the perfect balance to coexist together, without any pain, discomfort, or anxiety. You are here, breathing. And it feels good. You feel good.

Just breathe in. Hold it for a second, two. Then breathe out.

Breathe in. Breathe out.

The day has passed, you have survived. Give yourself a mental congratulation for all the hard work you do. You deserve it ; you deserve to be this calm now. You are allowed to relax your whole body, your mind.

The mind is a powerful thing. Just as it can bring stress and anxiety, it can also push them out and get you to profound tranquility. It can transport you to a different time, different place. If you believe it, you will see it.

With your breath still calm, imagine yourself sitting by the window. Looking outside, you notice how cloudy and grey it is. Rain is but moments away. You take a deep breath and breathe out slowly. Another in. And another out. Keep on breathing. Deeply, slowly, very calmly.

All of a sudden, a certain sound steals your attention. It is the sound of a raindrop hitting your window pane. Not long after, there is another one. And another. And yet another raindrop. The raindrops are getting more frequent and frequent, the sound getting louder and more intense. Soon enough, there are hundreds of these raindrops falling against your pane at once.

It is raining. You are still seated by the window, breathing calmly, enjoying the sound of the rain with your eyes closed. It is not overly heavy rain. If you were outside at this moment, you wouldn't be soaked immediately. Your windows are not being washed, but sprinkled.

Just sit by that window, enjoying the pitter-patter. The rain falling from a couple of thousands of meters of height – the air resisting their fall – the vibrations that they make when they hit your window.

Think about the rainfall and its monotonous and constant sound. Think about the nature. Why it rains. How it doesn't care where on when it will pour itself onto. It doesn't care about our problems, it doesn't care about anything. No circumstances involved, nothing. It is just pure nature doing its thing. Because it all comes down to it. Everything will pass – all of the troubles, all of the anxieties. This will stay the same, though. Nature will still go on. Life on earth will still go on.

Take a deep breath again, and breathe it out slowly through your nose. Continue breathing and think about the rainfall. Imagine it covering the streets, soaking the upper layer of the ground. Think about the people outside, hurrying to get to shelter, taking out their umbrellas. Think about that. I will now slowly count to 20, and you will stay focused on the rain – its sound, its power.

1, 2, 3, 4, 5, 6, 7, 8, 9, 10, 11, 12, 13, 14, 15, 16, 17, 18, 19, 20.

You like the rain. You find it soothing, relieving, liberating almost. You wish you were outside, closer to it. Feeling it on your skin.

All of a sudden, that's where you are. You are no longer by the window. You are standing outside, in the rain. You don't know how you got there; it doesn't matter at this point. Things shouldn't make sense in your mind right now. You should just be there. Present at that moment in your mind. Allow it to transport you places – allow it to bring experiences closer. Believe that it is so powerful.

You start walking down the street. The rain is falling down your cheeks, making your arms wet. Someone offers you an umbrella, but you don't need it. You would rather feel the nature on your skin. Enjoy the cool and wet touch that these drops leave on your skin.

You keep on walking and notice that there aren't that many people outside. It feels as though the whole street is yours. Reserved for you to enjoy the rain. So you keep on walking. Alone and calm. Breathing in the musky air – letting it draw positive feelings throughout your body. Making you feel good. Because it feels good to be walking in the rain.

Focus on your steps, how it feels to be pressing your feet onto this wet surface. Think about the smell. That earthy scent of rain moistening the ground. The fresh aroma hitting your nostrils. And you take it all in. You inhale deeply as though you want to breathe in the whole thing at once. Suck the whole scent out of the ground, enjoy the petrichor even more profoundly.

Breathe in. Breathe out.

Breathe in. Breathe out.

Feeling the rain on your skin.

Inhaling deeply. Exhaling slowly.

You keep on breathing, calmly, and slowly.

Breathe in. Breathe out.

As I count to 10, you keep on going down the street. Feeling the rain on your skin, enjoying its scent, feeling alive.

1, 2, 3, 4, 5, 6, 7, 8, 9, 10.

You have been walking for some time now. You are starting to get tired. Your body is becoming heavier. Each step is becoming harder and harder, while each breath gives you a lighter sensation. The steps become heavy, the breath lighter.

Breathe in. Breathe out.

Breathe in. Breathe out.

But it is not only your breath that it is getting lighter. The rain is also starting to lose its intensity. The raindrops that are hitting your skin now become less frequent. The whole mood seems brighter. Perhaps it is because the sun has started peeking from behind the clouds. Maybe it is all in your mind. You have become free of stress, free of unwanted thoughts, and you instantly feel brightened up. Lighter. Better. Calm. Relaxed.

Just breathing. Deeply and calmly. In and out.

Breathe in. Breathe out.

Breathe in. Breathe out.

Even though your entire body feels heavy, you keep on walking. And walking. And walking.

The rain is gone now, and the sun has taken over. Claiming its presence in a warm way on your skin. Drying up the wetness that the rain has left behind it. You are feeling warmer. Better.

Somehow, your journey is over, and you are back by the window. Settled in a comfortable position. With your eyes still closed.

You think about the rain and the sun. Their connection to your mood – anxious and relaxed. You think about the changes in nature. The shift that happens outside, as well as inside. Inside your mind, inside your body. We are all changing, growing, evolving.

You keep on breathing and allow your mind to simply drift off.

You feel calm and utterly at peace at this moment.

Allow the tranquility to spread throughout your whole being. Consuming all of you. Physically. Mentally.

Breathing in and out, deeply, and calmly, you have entered serenity.

Stay there. It feels good there. Your senses are all at peace. You are free.

Just breathe in and out. In and out. Allowing yourself to slowly doze off.

Dozing off.. relaxed and calm.

Just sliding… drifting… enjoying being in your own skin.

Existing…

Pre-Sleep Mindfulness Practice

Duration: 30 minutes

If meditating has been hard for you, or if you need more time to unwind, then that is probably because your days are too stressful. If that is the case, then, in addition to your bedtime story or sleep meditation, you should also do a thirty-minute mindfulness practice to knock down the stress. This will make you aware of your surroundings and be present at the moment, putting behind all of the thoughts and feelings that are not associated with this exact moment. That way, you can put yourself in a healthy pre-sleep mode, and will be able to drift away easily.

If your goal is to fall asleep quicker, then this mindfulness practice is best performed right before your bedtime routine. In addition, you can take advantage of this to put a top to your racing mind any time of the day.

Let's begin by finding you a comfortable spot. It can be a chair, a cushion, your sofa, or simply sit on the floor if that feels good for you. Do not close your eyes completely, keep them open halfway.

Now, take a deep breath. Do your best to focus all of your attention solely on the breath. Not so much on the breathing as an act – just noticing how you breathe in and out will not suffice. You need to really feel your breath. Feel the air coming in and leaving your body.

So, take a deep breath and hold it for some time. Two to three seconds will be enough. Let it out through your nose, very slowly.

Now again, breathe in deeply, but this time, focus on the breath that it is going in. Feel the air in your nostrils, how it feels when you inhale, how your abdominal area changes with the deep breath, how your chest rises while the lungs get expanded. When letting the breath out, notice the change in the chest and lungs – how they come down; be aware of how your nostrils feel when the air is flowing through them.

Again, take a deep breath in. Hold for two seconds. Breathe out.

Breathe in [pause]. Breathe out.

Breathe in. Wait, one, two. Breathe out.

Slowly, draw your attention from your breath to your surruondings. It is important for you to be fully aware, so that you can train your mind where to put your focus.

So, very gently, shift your focus from the breathing to your senses. Start with the smell. Bring your attention to what your nose can sense at this point. What kind of scent can be detected? Perhaps there is an air freshener in your room or a scented candle, maybe. Maybe your window is open and there is a slight breeze pushing the scent of the outside your way. Fresh grass, flowers, or perhaps a musky and earthy notes can be recognized. If you cannot detect anything, slowly bring your head closer to your shoulder. Feel the scent of your skin – a body lotion or cloth softener should leave aromatic notes for your nose to trace.

I will now slowly count to 10, and you will use this time to focus on this sense. Feel scent, but do not just notice it is there. Try to detect as many notes as you possibly can. In the meantime, keep breathing calmly and slowly.

1, 2, 3, 4, 5, 6, 7, 8, 9, 10.

Gently draw your attention back to the breath. Calm and slow. Breathe in. Breathe out. Just inhaling and exhaling. Feeling it in your nostrils, in your lungs. Breathe in. Breathe out.

Now, shift the focus to your ears. What can you hear at this very moment? Are there any noises? If you're not alone at home, focus on the chattering, or the sounds that are coming from the other room. Do not get into details – do not try to decipher, just know that they are there. Be aware.

Perhaps you've put on some relaxing music. Or there are some sounds coming from outside. Focus on that.

If you cannot hear anything, that is even better. Just focus on the silence. Place your attention there, and keep on breathing calmly. As I slowly count to 10, you will stay focused on the sound.

1, 2, 3, 4, 5, 6, 7, 8, 9, 10.

Return to your breath. Slowly and gently. Breathe in. Breathe out. Inhale and exhale. Another deep breath in. A slow breath out. In and out.

From your breath, place your attention on your eyes. They are open halfway, so focus on the things you can see. Do not open them widely, keep them as they are. Do not move your head either. Just keep you gaze straight ahead, looking at whatever's there in front of you. A wall, a window, a bed… it doesn't matter. Just kee your focus there, merely observing.

As I count to 10, breathe slowly, keeping your attention on your eyes.

1, 2, 3, 4, 5, 6, 7, 8, 9. 10.

Breathe in. Breathe out. Inhale and exhale. Returning your attention to your breath, but still, keep your eyes open halfway.

Gently. In and out. In and out. You breathe in slowly. Breathe in gently. In and out.

Now, very slowly, shift your focus from your breath to your mouth. Try to focus on the taste on your tongue. Perhaps you've eaten something before this practice, or you have chewing gum. Focus on what can be detected by your taste buds. Sweet, salty, sour, minty… whatever the taste is, keep your attention there. Stay focused on this sense while I slowly count to 10.

1, 2, 3, 4, 5, 6, 7, 8, 9, 10.

Now, breathe in deeply. And breathe out gently. Again, breathe in. Breathe out. Return your focus slowly to your breath. Placing all of your attention there. Just breathing in. And breathing out. In and out.

Calmly. Slowly. Feeling the air flowing through your nostrils and into your lungs. Then letting it go. Breathing in. And out. In and out.

Your attention is now on your breath. Try to shift it to your hands. Put your focus on your last sense – the sense of touch. Try to put your hands on your knees. See how the touch feels on your palms. If your knees are exposed, feel the skin on your palms. How does it feel? Once you touch your skin, you will notice a heat transfer taking place You will be able to feel a warmer and colder touch at the same time. See if you can recognize which of those come from your palm and which is the temperature of your knees? Are your hands colder than the knees?

If you are wearing pants or pajamas, focus on how the clothing material on your palms. If you need to, move your fingers gently, rubbing them against the clothing, Is it soft? Perhaps smooth? Think about this sensation, feeling it, becoming aware of it.

As I slowly count to 10, you will keep your attention on your touch, with your breath slow and calm.

1, 2, 3, 4, 5, 6, 7, 8, 9, 10.

Now that your attention is on your hands, do not shift it to your breath – keep it there. Don't focus on the touch now, but on your hands in general. Try to really feel them. Your palms, your fingers. How do they feel? Are they stiff? Heavy?

From there, draw your attention upward, noticing your lower arms, elbows, upper arms. Move your focus to your shoulders – see how this part of your body feels. Is there any tension there? Try to lower them or slightly throw them back,

Moving upward through your neck, scanning for stiffness there, go to your head. To break up any stressful knots in this upper part of your body, try to move your head around in circles, very gently and slowly, to relieve both your neck and head.

Put your focus on your face and see how it feels now. If a thought pops up, just notice it is there then shrug it off by returning your attention to your body.

From there, gently start going down, through the neck again, back to the shoulders, but this time, move to your chest. While there, take a deep breath and notice the movement. How it puffs up and deflates. If it feels too tense, try to take a couple of deep breaths to relieve it.

Breath in deeply Hold, one, two, three. Release slowly.

Repeat again.

Taking a deep breath. Hold, one, two, three. Breathe out slowly.

From there, move the attention to your abdomen and scan for tension there. Move to your pelvic, hips, then go down to your things, knees, scanning for tension. Move down to your calves, ankles, finishing the scan in your feet.

Go back to your breath now. Breathing in. Breathing out. In and out. Feel its presence, notice it is there.

While breathing calmly, slowly, open your eyes widely.

Spend the next minute just breathing and absorbing your surroundings. Wait a few moments before you get up and return to getting ready for bed.

Massage-Like Sleep Therapy

Duration: 20 minutes

A long back rub and a good foot massage before sleep? Yes, please! We all love the relaxing feeling we get when someone is massaging our body, but we can agree that it is impossible to have one every single night. Or is it, really?

With this 20-minute meditation, you will explore the magical touch a good massage leaves on our body and feel just as relaxed at the end, even though this rub will exist only in your mind.

With no time to waste, I will now ask you to lie down in your bed, not as you would for an actual massage, but to get ready as if you were about to fall asleep. Make sure you are comfortable and close your eyes. Let's begin.

Start by relaxing yourself with a calm and slow breath. Breathe in slowly. Breathe out. In and out. You are feeling the air through your nostrils, in your lungs. And out of your chest, through your nostrils again.

Breathing in. Breathing out.

Now, imagine yourself getting a massage. Imagine a pair of hands going deep in your back. Feel their thumbs sinking in, pressing deeply into your flesh, looking for tight knots that they can untangle.

In the meantime, you are breathing slowly, enjoying the rubbing. You are getting used to the touch. More and more. Feeling relaxed. It almost feels as though you can see the tension disappear.

One by one, these hands seem to be magically breaking up the knots on your back.

It started gently and slowly, but now the massage has taken on a more vigorous intensity. The pressure is stronger, the touch goes deeper. And deeper. The hands are kneading the tissue of your muscles in a deep and strong way, but it feels so good. Although the pressure is firm, the touch feels magical. It doesn't hurt – quite the contrary. It relieves any pain or tension piled up in knots inside.

Try to really feel these smooth strokes. They are warming up your back, applying pressure that relaxes. Relives tension. Gets rid of tightness. Focus on this feeling. How it would really feel if you were actually getting a massage.

Imagine a pair of hands gliding over your back, pulling the muscles, leaving pressure that soothes not only your back but your entire body.

Now scan your back for tightness; if there is an area that feels tighter than the rest of the back, imagine an elbow pressing into it. Feel the circular movements of the imaginery elbow making the spot softer and softer. Leaving you with a relaxing sensation.

Don't forget to breathe calmly. Your breath is the most important thing in this practice, so make sure you are breathing in and out in a very calm and relaxed way.

Breathe in. Breathe out. Feeling the back softening.

Breathe in. Breathe out. A relaxing sensation all over it.

Breathe in. Breathe out.

Now move your focus to your neck. Feel a hand pressing into it, making the tissue more pileable. Relieving you from stiffness.

As the hand moves to one of your arms, you can immediately feel the neck becoming softer, more relaxed.

Now it is your arms' turn. Starting at your upper left arm, imagine a pair of hands applying gentle strokes downward, toward your hand. Pressing into the tissue, now the pressure is mild, the pace slow. You can feel the hands squeezing gently, living a soothing sensation that lingers long after the touch is gone.

The hands now move to your hand and the fingers, rubbing and relieving pressure. It relaxes you. So soothing.

Now the next arm. Feel the same pressure, the same sensation. Squeezing, applying pressure, relieving.

Don't forget about the breath. Breathe in. Breathe out.

Breathe in. And breathe out. Slowly and gently. In and out.

Now focus on your legs. Feel your thighs getting a massage. First, the left one – mild pressure there warms up the tissue. The strokes that pull the muscles leave a relaxing feeling that makes you feel good.

Now the right one. With the same pressure an method, the tissue is kneaded and lifted. Softening up, relieving.

Feel the hands go down to your lower legs, your calves. Feel the gliding pressure there. Starting slowly, then transitioning to a more vigorous pace. Pressing into the skin, pulling the flash, gently and comfortably.

Breathe in. Breathe out.

Feel the pressure in your legs. Feel them relaxing. Notice a tingling sensation there. It feels good. You feel good.

Now gently, move to your feet. Imagine your left foot is being rubbed. Feel the circular movement there, the fingers pressing into your feet, relieving the pressure that your long day has left. Now, feel the other one relaxing as well. The gentle pressure there, the squeezing that soothes.

And take another breath again. Slowly and calmly. Breathing in. And breathing out.

In and out. A breath goes in. A breath goes out.

Breathe in. Breathe out.

I will now count to 10, and you will stay focused on your body as a whole. Feel a relaxing sensation flowing through the back, neck, arms, legs, feet. Feel it everywhere. Soothing and liberating. You are softening up. The tightness disappearing. The hands are no longer on your body, but you can still feel the touch. Gentle and tingling. Helping you ease your whole being. Focus on this and try to really feel your body relieving from pressure.

1, 2, 3, 4, 5, 6, 7, 8, 9, 10.

Feel your body becoming heavier, sinking into your bed. Relaxed and so heavy, it feels like you are drowning in your sheets. They are swallowing you up, slowly, and gently. You are heavy, cannot stay on the surface.

So, you give in.

Going deeper and deeper.

You let go of everything.

Your body is so relaxed.

The sensation calms you down, mentally as well.

Your mind is starting to drift away… letting go

You are feeling tired. Heavy and sleepy.

Don't fight the feeling. Allow it to consume you.

Sleepy. Dozing off. Sleep…

Walking with the Rainbows – Guided Visualizing Sleep Mediation

Duration: 30 minutes

There is something magical about the rainbows. Perhaps it is the spectrum of their colors or the fact that they magically appear when rain and sun join their forces. Or that they always happen to be covered in mist. You just cannot help but think a magic wand created them.

But besides their fairytale-like look, there is also something soothing about these colorful things we see in the sky. We will now take advantage of their relaxing look to get ourselves into a calm state that will knock down pressure and anxiety, and puts us to sleep.

First, before we begin, make sure that you settle into a comfortable position in your bed, placing yourself in such a way that will allow you to easily fall asleep. Assuming you have turned off all electronics and distractions, you can now close your eyes and let me guide you through this magical journey.

Let's start by detaching yourself from the present realness that surrounds you. We can easily do this by simply focusing on your breath. Not just on the way you breathe – it is not enough to just know that we are breathing in and out. But really put your attention on the breath. How it enters your body, and the way in which it goes out of it.

So, take a deep breath. While it is filling your lungs, feel its presence there. Hold for two seconds. Then slowly release it through your nose, noticing how it feels in your nostrils.

Take another deep breath. Hold it in for two to three seconds. Release slowly.

And another. Only this time, do not feel it in your lungs, but focus on your nostrils, how they feel when the air is flowing in. When releasing the breath now, don't focus on the nostrils, but shift the attention to the lungs now – feel them shrink.

So, a deep breath goes in. We're feeling it flowing through the nostrils. One, two, we are breathing out, focusing on our lungs and how they shrink in size.

Another breath in. One, two, three. A breath out.

A breath in [pause]. A breath out.

Now, imagine yourself opening your eyes. You will not open them, but just imagine yourself doing so. You open your eyes, and you find yourself outside. You don't know the place you are at. You have never been here before, you are sure of it. And yet, it somehow feels familiar.

Maybe it is because of the lush meadow. Or old, shadow-giving trees. Or your favorite flowers being sewn all across the thick green blanket. Whatever it is, it feels good to be in this place.

You start walking ahead. And walking. And walking. Your breath is composed, undisturbed. You are feeling calm. It is so peaceful there. And so you are walking. And walking. And walking ahead.

Breathing in. And breathing out.

Breathe in. Breathe out.

Inhaling calmly. And exhaling slowly.

You continue on the path. After a while, you notice that no matter how long you are walking, the meadow remains as lush and as rich with flowers as when you took your first step.

The weather is sunny, but not hot – ideal for long walks. It is almost noon; you know that by the sun's place in the sky, but somehow, you feel as though you can be walking like this until sunset.

Enjoying the sun's warmth on your skin, the green fields in front of you, breathing in the floral scents, you continue walking. Step by step, and slowly, you continue ahead.

Breathing in. Breathing out.

In and out. In and out.

You feel a drop of water on your cheek. You look up, but there aren't that many clouds. Could it really be raining? Then another drop meets your arm, and another, and another one. The rain has indeed started to fall.

It is not a heavy rain though, it doesn't affect your perfect walk in any way. If you're being honest, you are thankful for it. The raindrops leave a cool touch on your face and arms, making your walk even more enjoyable. But that is not the only thing you're enjoying.

All of a sudden, in front of you, a giant rainbow appears. It is not only visible, but it seems that as you keep on walking and walking, its colors become clearer and brighter.

Focus on each of the colors individually. Starting with the first color – red, put your attention there. What this color means. What it represents. Think about things that you like that are red in color. Visualize a red rose, cutting a ripe watermelon, a red heart, strawberries… The blood that is running through your veins at the moment. Think about what the color looks like.

I will now slowly count to 10, and you will use that time to think about all things red. Just breath calmly and slowly.

1, 2, 3, 4, 5, 6, 7, 8, 9, 10.

Moving to the second color – orange. Think about oranges, carrots, watching the sunrise in your favorite place… Do not obsess over the details. Just think of whatever you can associate the color orange with. Just let these thoughts come to your mind, naturally.

Meanwhile, keep on breathing in and out. In and out. Orange flowers, orange sweets… whatever comes to your mind.

1, 2, 3, 4, 5, 6, 7, 8, 9, 10.

Think about the third color of the spectrum – yellow. Think of the sun, lemons, sunflowers… Whatever you think it's yellow. Don't get into specifics. Even if the object that comes to your mind is not yellow – it is okay. Just let these yellow things float in your mind, while breathing slowly. Keep doing this for the next 15-20 seconds.

1, 2, 3, 4, 5, 6, 7, 8, 9, 10.

Visualize green. Lush green grass like the meadow that it's all around you at the moment. Green avocados, lime, leaves… Spend the next seconds breathing calmly, thinking about things that are green in color.

1, 2, 3, 4, 5, 6, 7, 8, 9, 10.

Now think of blue and indigo colors. Think of the sky. How it goes from light and bright when sunny to dark when the night creeps in. Think of the deep blue ocean. Of the blue eyes of a person you love. I will count to 10 again, and you will use that time to breathe slowly and think of all things blue.

1, 2, 3, 4, 5, 6, 7, 8, 9, 10.

Finally, think of the color purple. Imagine lush lavender fields, blueberries, violets, other purple flowers… Just keep your eyes closed, and let your imagination bring you these purple objects close to you. Breathe slowly. In and out. Imagining purple.

1, 2, 3, 4, 5, 6, 7, 8, 9, 10.

Now observe the rainbow as a whole. See these vibrant colors in front of you, so alive. The light and color put you into a relaxing mood that it is almost sedating. But you keep on going. The rainbow is still there. Guiding your way, encouraging you to keep going. Ahead and ahead. Slowly and at peace. Feeling so relaxed.

Focus on the rainbow, on how it spreads over the pathway you are walking on. The more and more you keep on going, the brighter and larger it becomes. You almost feel like you could catch the rainbow.

So you are getting closer and closer. Your feet are getting heavier and heavier. You can almost see the reflection of the vibrant colors on the pathway. Is it real? Or is it just a mirage?

Getting closer and closer. You are almost there. Keep on walking.

So heavy. So relaxed.

Finally, you come to the end. You are standing right below the rainbow. The pathway ends here, so you cannot go any further.

Feeling heavy, you lie down below these vibrant colors. Allowing them to wrap you up with security and deep relaxation.

So heavy, you feel your whole body sinking.

Deeper and deeper.

Almost reaching another atmosphere.

Drifting away…

Into deep sleep…

Into a state of equilibrium…

Almost there… sleep!

15-Minute Self-Hypnosis for Sleep

Duration: 15 minutes

Lull yourself to sleep in just 15 minutes with this self-hypnosis technique that will force your mind to stay focus on one thing and one thing only. By practicing this technique on a regular basis, you will gain experience in self-hypnosis that will help you find a healthy sleeping pattern that will practically knock out insomnia.

Let's start by wearing comfortable clothes and settling into a comfortable position you can fall asleep from. Get rid of any distractions, and close your eyes.

Take a deep breath and then breathe out slowly. Take another one. And breathe it out.

Breathe in again. Deeply and slowly. Out through the nose.

Keep breathing deeply, and with each deep breath, imagine yourself going deeper and deeper.

Imagine the count of 10 – 1, 2, 3, 4, 5, 6, 7, 8, 9, 10.

One being awake and alert, and ten being the point when you will fall into deep sleep. Think of these two numbers, as they will matter the most to you. 1 – awake, 2- asleep. Think of the other numbers in between, 2 through 9, as steps that you need to pass in order to get from the beginning to the end. From 1 to 10.

ONE – You are wake, lying in your bed with your eyes closed. You are in a comfortable position, wanting to fall asleep. Needing sleep. Craving rest.

Take a deep breath, as deep as you can. Hold it for a second, two. As you are breathing out, slowly through your nose, imagine yourself climbing dow one step.

TWO – Now you have come lower. Remember that sleep is at number 10, so you have eight more steps to go. Let this thought guide your way.

Keep breathing deeply. As deep as you can. Now, let the breath out very slowly, imagining yourself climbing down to number three.

THREE – You can already feel your body becoming a little bit heavier. You are still alert, but you have definitely started to fall down into a different dimesion. Somewhere between your dreams and the reality.

Take another deep breath. Let it all the way in, deep within your lungs. Let go very slowly, while climbing down another step.

FOUR – Can you feel how the tension has already started to become less and less noticeable? You take another deep breath, getting yourself even deeper.

FIVE – You have gone hallway now, sleep is almost within reach. Feel your arms getting heavy, your legs sinking deep into the bed.

Take another deep breath. Hold it for a second, two. Now, let it out through the nose

SIX – You can feel your mind detaching from the present reality now. It is a good and calming feeling. You take another deep breath. When exhaling, you come down, even deeper.

SEVEN – You feel your whole body getting tired, your senses have already started to turn off. You take another deep breath, and you let it out slowly, feeling your whole body going deeper and deeper.

EIGHT – You have two more steps to go. Your eyelids are so heavy that you feel like you cannot open them, even if you try. It is a similar sensation like that when you wake up early in the morning, with glued eyes, needing more sleep.

You take a deep breath, and breathe out slowly.

NINE – Your whole body feels heavy now. You are heavy and tired, but surprisingly, you feel lighter. So light, that you think you are not even lying in bed. You feel like a feather, just floating deeper and deeper down.

With a deep breath in and out, you go even lower.

TEN – You have arrived. Your eyes are tired. Your body has already given in. Just let it be as it is. Forget about everything. Relax. Drifting away… Ready to sleep…

Sliding Down to Sleep – Guided Meditation

Duration: 20 minutes

Welcome to this 20-minute guided meditation. Tonight, we will visit a marvelous place that will unleash the child within you. At the start of this meditation, we will leave behind all of our thoughts and anxieties and climb high. Once we reach the top, we will slide down a giant slide that will take us to serenity – a deep state of pure relaxation that will allow you to sleep for at least 6-8 good hours. Ready for the ride?

Before we begin, make sure that you are comfortable. It is important that you do not be distracted or feel any discomfort during this practice, so you can easily fall asleep. Find a sleeping position that you can fall asleep from, and close your eyes.

Just like all other practices, start this one by focusing on your breath. That way, you can relax snap out of the reality that is surrounding you and allow yourself to enter a place in your mind that will help you relax.

So, take a deep breath. Feel the air through your nostrils and inside your lungs. Keep the breath for two seconds, then let it out slowly, through your nose.

Another deep breath goes in. A slow breath goes out.

Breathing in deeply. Breathing out slowly

Breathing in And breathing out.

In and out. In and out.

Imagine yourself standing in a room filled with all of your thoughts and anxieties. Your fears, Your uncertainties. The things that make you doubt yourself. The unimportant things that pop up inside your head, uninvited. All the things that keep you up at night are there. Spend a few moments observing them. Imagine yourself starting them directly at their face. Just observing – not getting into details. You know that they are there – you acknowledge their presence.

I will now count to 10, and you will observe the thoughts that pop into your mind without getting into the specifics.

1, 2, 3, 4, 5, 6, 7, 8, 9, 10.

The room is extremely small – claustrophobic even. There are no doors, only a staircase on the wall in front of you. Leaving all of your thoughts and worries behind, you have started climbing up. One step, twp steps, three steps, four steps, five… You look down, and you see your thoughts and emotions are left there – in the room. You did not take them with you – they cannot affect you anymore. It is just you and the stairs at this point. So go up. Six steps, seven steps, eight steps, nine steps, ten steps…

Eleven steps, twelve steps, thirteen steps, fourteen steps…

With each step, your legs are feeling heavier.

Fifteen steps, sixteen steps, seventeen steps, eighteen steps, nineteen steps, twenty steps…

Heavier and heavier.

Twenty-one steps, twenty-two steps, twenty-three steps, twenty-four steps…

Feel your whole body getting tired. You don't know how much more of these steps there is, but you have to go up. There is no other way out of this. Heavier and heavier, you continue.

Twenty-five steps, twenty-six steps, twenty-seven steps, twenty-eight steps…

You think you cannot go any higher, but you surprise yourself with your strength. You muster it all, and head up.

Twenty-nine steps, thirty steps, thirty-one steps, thirty-two steps, thirty-three steps, thirty-four steps…

You look up, but you cannot see anything there. Just the wall and the steps. You are getting tired and tired, but you have to keep on moving.

Thirty-five steps thirty-six steps, thirty-seven steps, thirty-eight steps, thirty-nine steps, forty steps…

You take a deep breath, making a stop to rest. You breathe in deeply, and you breathe out slowly. A deep breath in. A slow breath out. Once again. In deeply, out slowly. Breathe in. Breathe out. Let's keep on going.

Forty-one steps, forty-five steps, forty-six steps…

You can see the end is coming close. You can see where this staircase ends, but you don't know where it will lead you.

Forty-seven steps, forty-eight steps… almost there…

Forty-nine steps, fifty steps.

You are finally there. Your feet are so tired that you need to sit down. You are feeling so heavy, you can barely move. You don't know if you have the strength to keep on going. Luckily, you won't have to. Once you look around, you see that there is a slide that will lead you down. Down to serenity, down to a deep state of relaxation.

Without any time to think, you push yourself down it, allowing the slide to lead you into the unknown.

Sliding down you cannot help but feel liberating. The breeze in your hair, dancing on your skin. The force pulling you downward, the will to get to the other side of the slide as fast as you can.

Going down, you feel your whole body taking on a tingling sensation. A strange force fills you up, making you even heavier and heavier.

It is hard to even keep your eyes open. You are struggling with staying alert and letting go completely. But don't fight it. Just let yourself be entirely consumed by this moment. This magnificent feeling of sliding down.

Feel the heaviness rise, your eyelids shutting tightly, your body becoming so heavy that it feels like you're sinking into the slide. Almost there.

Any moment now.

Just let yourself be.

Let yourself feel this heavy and deep relaxation taking over, claiming its presence.

Let it take over.

Allow it to lull to sleep.

Because you are sleepy. You want to rest. You deserve to relax.

About to doze off…

… and fall into a sound sleep.

Conclusion

Thank you for reading (or listening to) this book and for sticking with me to the very end. I hope that these bedtime stories and meditation practices will help you find the well-deserved rest that was robbed from you by your racing mind or restless nature.

Try them all and see which one is designed to fit your needs the best. I'd love to hear all about your experiences!

Sweet dreams!

Bedtime Stories for Stressed Out Adults: Relaxing Sleep Stories, Guided Mindfulness Meditations & Self-Hypnosis For Deep Sleep, Overcoming Anxiety, Insomnia & Stress Relief

By Meditation Made Effortless

Contents

1. Morning at the Seaside Cottage (60 Minutes) 1
2. Sheltering In The Book Store (50 Minutes) 4
3. The Night Train North (70 Minutes) 6
4. The Sleepy Mountain (50 Minutes) 9
5. The Night Sky (50 Minutes) 11
6. A Walk Along the Canal (80 Minutes) 13
7. A Walk Through The Magic Garden (60 Minutes) 16
8. Picnic Near the Waterfall (50 Minutes) 19
9. A Night On Your Paradise Island (70 Minutes) 21
10. A Trip Down the River (60 Minutes) 24

© **Copyright 2019 - All rights reserved.**

The content contained within this book may not be reproduced, duplicated or transmitted without direct written permission from the author or the publisher.

Under no circumstances will any blame or legal responsibility be held against the publisher, or author, for any damages, reparation, or monetary loss due to the information contained within this book; either directly or indirectly.

Legal Notice:

This book is copyright protected. This book is only for personal use. You cannot amend, distribute, sell, use, quote or paraphrase any part, or the content within this book, without the consent of the author or publisher.

Disclaimer Notice:

Please note the information contained within this document is for educational and entertainment purposes only. All effort has been executed to present accurate, up to date, and reliable, complete information. No warranties of any kind are declared or implied. Readers acknowledge that the author is not engaging in the rendering of legal, financial, medical or professional advice.

1. Morning at the Seaside Cottage (60 Minutes)

Hello and welcome to this sleep story. Start by making yourself nice and comfortable in bed. Allow any thoughts or feeling from the day to drift away. Give your mind the chance to open itself up to the experience it's about to have. When you are ready, just allow your eyes to gently close. Fully experience how comfortable you feel under the covers. How nice it is to just spread out and have this time just for yourself. Sleep is a precious thing and should be treated as such. This is your time to relax and allow your mind and body to recharge for tomorrow.

Start by taking in a few deep breaths. And then allow the air to leave your body slowly. Do this a few times until you can feel the relaxing benefits. Then just allow yourself to breath naturally as you start your journey to the seaside cottage.

There is a beautiful cottage by the sea. It's right on the edge of the beach, giving the occupier an amazing view of the sea and the distant horizon. The cottage is old but still looks warm and inviting. You can tell that it has been home to families who have grown up there and who have appreciated everything that the cottage has to offer. Just by being here for a day, you can make yourself feel so much more relaxed and happy. So carefree and without any worries.

This is an amazing place to come to after you have spent the day at the beach. After taking in the beautiful sun beaming down on you, there is nothing better than heading to the seaside cottage, getting warm underneath a blanket and sitting by a nice log fire. Then you could sit on the porch and look up at the amazing night sky. It's incredible how when you're in a place like this, undisturbed by artificial lights of any kind, that you can see just how amazing the sky at night can be. How you can just gaze up for hours on end and allow your mind to drift off, thinking about what might be out there. About the new worlds you could be gazing at.

While the night's at the seaside cottage are amazing, nothing really can compare with the early mornings. If you are awake for sunrise, you can watch the beautiful morning sun slowly rising over the sea. Many people like to make themselves a nice cup of coffee and then sit on the deck and just watch the sun rise. Watch the orange colour spread over the sea in the distance until you can see the top of the sun poking out over the gentle waves. And then just watch as it continues to rise. And you can hear the seagulls greeting it good morning as it rises.

It always feels so comfortable on the cottage deck first thing in the morning. Even though it is a lot cooler than it can be during the day, it still feels a comfortable temperature. A nice steady breeze comes up from the sea and you can hear the gentle waves flowing over the sand. You can see the seagulls flying around, getting ready for all the visitors that will be coming to the beach in the hopes that they can get hold of some leftover picnic food.

The waves always seem so much calmer in the morning. You can walk along the beach in bare feet and allow the water to wash over you. The water will come up to the top of your ankle sometimes but the strength of the waves never feel like they could cause you problems. Instead you can stand there and allow the water to gently wash over you. The sea water can feel so cool and calming. If it has been a particularly warm night in the cottage, this can be amazing way to cool down a little. To just stand there, close your eyes, and fully the experience the sensations that the sea water brings as it washes over your feet. How you can feel the water weaving through your toes. How you can hear the waves around you and how they sound so much louder than they feel. You could just stand there for hours. Just feeling the rising sun becoming warmer and warmer against your skin.

You can then go for a walk along the beach near the cottage as the sun continues to rise. And when you do, you can take a moment to think about the magic of this place and what it means to you. This place is so wonderful and calming that all the troubles and struggles of life can simply wash away. It can almost feel like all the things that have been making you feel stressed or anxious have been carried away by the sea water and it flowed over your feet. This is an amazing place and it is here just for you. This is somewhere where you can truly let go and allow yourself to have a moment of peace and quiet. A place where you can totally relax and allow all of those life worries to drift away to sea. Until you can no longer see them in the distant horizon.

If on the walk back to the cottage you are coming from the south side, you can truly see what a magnificent little building it is. You can see it's made of wood but you know it has to be strong wood. This cottage has been here for so long. It has withstood the blasts of storms and sand battering the sides. It has managed to hold off all of that for so long. It's no wonder then that when you step inside after coming back from a walk, you can feel so perfectly safe.

After going for a walk and standing in the sea, it always feels nice to have a warm shower. Just to allow all of the sand and the salt crystals left behind by the sea to wash off your body. When you step out of the shower you feel so warm and comfortable. Then you can make yourself another cup of coffee and go back out onto the deck.

It's always amazing to sit on the porch during the early mornings at the seaside cottage. Just to sit there with a book and a coffee and just allowing yourself to have some time to yourself. In the modern world, it can always feel like you can't have moments of peace. Even when you are by yourself, you could still be receiving messages on your phone about work or something that is demanding your attention. But here, at the seaside cottage, nothing needs your attention. This is a place where you can truly relax and not worry about having to do anything.

You can just sit back, drink your coffee and read your book as you feel the sun rising. And even though you have had two cups of coffee, you still could allow yourself to drift off for a morning sleep. That's how relaxing this place can be. That's how much mental and physical freedom you can have in this place.

After reading a few chapters of your book, you put it down on the small table beside you. You finish the last of your coffee and then you lean back in your chair. Then, you just allow your eyes to gently close. You enjoy the feeling of the morning sun caressing your skin. You enjoy the sound of the seagulls in the distance. You enjoy the sound of the gentle waves as they crash against the sand. You fully appreciate how this wonderful serenity feels. And with that in mind, you are now able to just allow yourself to drift off to sleep, fully appreciating the amazing feeling you get simply by sitting on the porch of the seaside cottage.

2. Sheltering In The Book Store (50 Minutes)

Hello and welcome to tonight's sleep story. Tonight, we are going to be taking a trip to the book store. But before we can begin perusing the shelves looking for the next novel to read, we need to make ourselves nice and comfortable. So, climb into bed and make yourself feel warm and comfortable under the covers. Allow your head to be held by place by gravity on the pillow. Take in some deep breaths and then slowly breathe out. Do this a few times until you notice that the tension you might have been holding in your body has started to drift away. When you feel nice and comfortable, just allow yourself to breathe naturally. Now that you are ready, we can start out story.

If you have ever been caught in a downpour whilst walking down the street, you will know what a relief it is is to find a shop that is inviting enough to allow you to shelter. This book store we are about to enter is just one such place. At the moment, it is raining heavily and you are running down the street with your jacket held over your head to try and protect yourself. It's only been raining for a matter of seconds and already you know that you are going to be drenched by this downpour if you don't get shelter soon. This is when you notice the book shop just at the bottom of the road., You run down as quick as you can, obviously making sure that you don't slip along the way. And then you dart inside the shop and shut the door behind you.

As you walked in, you noticed the large windows the shop has facing out into the street. In the windows there are a wide range of books, from recent releases to some of the year's best sellers. The windows also display some of the finest old books, some of which could tell whole stories just by looking at their worn and battered covers.

This book shop is always open late. Which is lucky as the sun is now starting to set and the night is starting to close in. This doesn't effect the rain however, which continues to hammer down. You can hear the rain clattering against the large windows. The clattering becomes louder even now and then when the wind picks up a little.

Outside, you see the street lamps are starting to come on. They cast an orange light down on the wet pavement outside. The street lamp just outside the shop comes on now and illuminates in the books in the window, almost like they now have their own personal spotlight.

Above your head, you notice that the shop has a skylight as well. You look at it for a moment and watch the rain clattering against it. It's satisfying to watch the rain coming down, knowing that none of the rain will be able to make you uncomfortable and wet. You listen to the sound of the rain becoming heavier as the rain drops begin to mix with hail. You get the feeling you might be in here for a while, but you feel okay about that. There are certainly much worse places to be stuck during a heavy rain fall.

Just in the corner, you spot a comfortable looking leather chair. You can imagine that when people are visiting this store, they will frequently take a book they find interesting from the shelf and then sit down and enjoy flicking through it in comfort for a moment. You can imagine yourself taking an armful of books from the shelves and just sitting their and flicking through them for hours on end.

Next to the chair is a table on wheels and a sign that says you can leave any books that you have picked up there. You like this feature as it means you don't have to painstakingly remember where every single book you have picked up belongs. But then you think that if you owned this shop, this feature would be for you just as much as it is for the customers. If the owner of the shop is anything like you, then they would relish the thought of being able to walk around this shop with the trolley of books, finding where to put them back on the shelf. What a wonderful opportunity it would be to reacquaint yourself with all the knowledge and the stories that are available under this one roof.

In the other corner of the room, you can see Peter, the owner of the store. Peter is known in this area as being one of the nicest people you could ever meet. Always impeccably dressed in a suit with a waistcoat, you will always find him sat in the corner by his desk, reading one of the many books that have been dropped off with him for donations. It is said that Peter has read every single book that has ever been in that shop and the amount of knowledge he has gathered over the years could fill three libraries.

As always with customers, Peter greets you with a smile and tells you to have a look around and take your time. He says that you should make yourself comfortable so then you don't have to brave the rain until it calms. You thank him and take the opportunity to have a look over the shelves.

It's surprising because this doesn't seem like a large book shop, but it feels like every subject is represented here. As you pass the history section, you can see all the different subsections labelled perfectly. Victorian history. Tudor history. Chinese history. Even Icelandic history. You decide that you would like to sit down and have a look through some of these books. You take three or four from the shelf and then move over to the chair in the corner.

As you sit down, you fully appreciate the support that the chair is giving you. Even though you have only just sat down, you already feel incredibly comfortable and relaxed. It feels like the chair was designed exclusively to support your body. You get nice and comfortable and pick up the first book.

As you pick up the book, you look up to the skylight again and watch the continuing rain and hail. For you, this downpour could last all night. It would not matter to you one bit. You can't think of anywhere else you would like to be sheltering from the rain.

Just as you sink in the chair a little more, Peter walks over with a hot cup of tea. He places it on the table next to you and says that he figured you would need that to warm yourself up after being caught in that rain. You thank him and he tells you to take your time and enjoy the selection of books you have chosen. He says he has read them and would recommend all of them.

Peter smiles and then walks back over to his desk and continues reading his book. You take a sip from the tea he has given you. Even that first sip feels so comforting and warming. You can feel the effects drifting through your body. Any signs of tension or discomfort in your body now slowly floating away.

You sink a little deeper into the seat and pick up that first book again and start reading. And then, as you turn the book over to the next page, you find yourself slowly drifting off. Just gradually falling asleep now as you read. You take another sip of tea and feel the warmth and calming effects flowing through you. And then you gently close your eyes and drift off. And as you do, all you can hear is the sound of the rain and hail clattering down on the skylight above you.

3. The Night Train North (70 Minutes)

Welcome to tonight's sleep story. Tonight, we are going to be taking the night train to the north. So before we begin, making sure that you are nice and comfortable in bed. Get settled under the covers and get into a comfortable position. Then when you are ready, gently close your eyes. Allow any thoughts you might be having to drift away. Enjoy the feeling of having a calm mind. There is nothing that you need to think about right now. All you have to do is get comfortable and relax. Take in a deep breath and then release the air slowly. Do this a couple more times. Enjoy how doing this makes you feel. When you start to feel more comfortable, just allow your breathing to return to its natural rhythm.

Are you ready? Good. Then we will begin our story.

The sun has just started to set as you take your seat on that night train. You look out of the window and you can see the sun gently starting to set. It's just starting to disappear behind the station where the last few passengers are waiting for the next train. You hear the wheels starting to whir into motion as you slowly start to be carried away from the station. You watch the scenery around you as your train starts to pick up more speed. The station where you started is already starting to disappear into the distance. As you take in your surroundings, you can hear the gentle sound of the engine working. Speeding up the train more and more as you gently start to move forwards. Just a gentle forward motion slowly taking you down the tracks.

As you look out of the window, you can see the grassy hills and the distant river. You can see the sunset being reflected in the calm water as the sun continues to set. The only thing that can distract you from this view is the occasional glistening of the lights on the track, curling in the distance. You can see all the yellows and the reds of the shining lights. You're gradually heading towards them and they look inviting.

As the train moves through the hills, a rainfall starts. It's very gentle. You can hear the rain tapping gently on the roof of the train. It's a soothing sound. In the distance, you can see the drops of water gently landing on the distant river. You watch the drops hitting the water. How the sound of the rain hitting the roof of the train almost matches the rhythm of the rain hitting the river. It sounds almost like you are listening to a gentle song. Like you are being serenaded on your journey.

Your seat on the train is comfortable. It has a tall back and plenty of legroom so you can stretch out and relax. You have a table in front of you and there is a little sign saying that you can connect to the wi-fi if you wish. But you don't want to. All you want to do is fully take in this moment and the feelings that you have on this journey.

You look around. You take in the surroundings on the train and what you can see outside. You notice the rain picking up and the small drops of water hitting the window next to you. You watch the small beads of water as they start to move down the glass. Then as the train picks up a little more speed, you notice the little drops moving to the side as well. Struggling to cling to the glass as the wind and the speed of the train try and blow the beads of rain away. You watch this happening as you settle a little more into your seat. It feels so comfortable and warm.

You're moving through beautiful fields now. Every blade of grass looks vibrantly green and inviting. You enjoy feeling like you are far from civilization now. Almost like this train journey is just for you and you alone. You notice that the rain clouds are now starting to move over the night sky as the sun continues to disappear over the horizon.

As you watch the sun slowly disappearing, you can see a herd of cows grazing in the field far in the distance. There aren't any human beings around. You look and you can't see any other people for miles around. It feels like you have found a quiet corner of the world just for yourself. Like you have created a special place where you can be free of your stresses and anxieties. Where you can be free of anything that has been on your mind for a while. You enjoy the feeling of having a clear mind as you watch the cows. The fields. The gentle rainfall against the window.

You look out of the opposite window and all you can see is the open ocean. In the distance, you can see some big fishing vessels, coming back in to shore with their catches from the day. Even though the train is moving fast and in the opposite direction to the vessels, it still looks like they are gently floating away at a slow pace. It takes several minutes before they disappear out of view of the window.

As you look at the ocean, you notice how smooth it looks. It's almost like it's reacting to the setting sun and is settling down for a comfortable night. As you look at this, a gentle voice comes over the tannoy and announces that you will soon be arriving at the first station on your route. The station stands out against the picturesque surroundings and doesn't seem to have any connection to a town or a city. It's strange seeing a station like this in the middle of nowhere. Perhaps it is not surprising then that when the train comes to a stop at the station, you can only see two people getting onto the train. They both run frantically, hoping they will not get too wet moving onto the train from under the small roof covering the tiny platform.

The station is made almost entirely of wood that has been painted red. A large clock hangs from the front of the station, making sure that no passengers are ever stuck for the current time. You look into the waiting room, illuminated by the two or three ceiling lights. You imagine that if the train wasn't here, chances are the light in that waiting room would be the only light around for miles. You imagine being able to see it all the way back at the calm river that you passed a while ago.

As you look at the waiting room, you see a women in a raincoat. She's reading a book she's holding in one hand while cradling a cup of hot coffee in the other. You can see the steam rising from the cup. She takes a sip and you can see that it's comforting her and making her feel a little warmer. Given how late it is getting, you know that this woman must be preparing herself for a long journey if she's having coffee at this hour. Perhaps even longer than the journey you're on now. You have no doubt that she will be looking forward to her trip just as much as you have been looking forward to yours. You get the feeling that all she will need is her book and perhaps another cup of coffee to keep her warm as she watches the scenery go by. And perhaps watches the rain hitting the window next to her. You watch her turn from her book as she watches the last bit of the sun disappear over the horizon before settling down to her book once again.

Your train starts to rhythmically move again. One of the new passengers walks through your carriage. They look at you and smile and nod. You smile and nod back at them as they walk past you. A beverage carriage comes down the aisle and inspired by the man you saw, you ask for a cup of tea. The person serving you smiles as they fill a cup with hot, steamy water. They remove the tea bag and add a little milk. They then put it down on the table in front of you with a smile and say that they hope you will enjoy your night on the train.

You notice the comfortable blanket that you have by your side. You take a sip of tea and enjoy the feeling of the hot liquid as it moves from your throat through your body. It's a nice comfortable feeling. You can feel any tension that you have been holding slowly starting to drift away. This train journey is exactly what you need. Making you feel so comfortable and relaxed. So free of stress and anxiety. So comfortable.

You take the blanket and start wrapping yourself up in it. Then you take another sip of tea. You feel the relaxation and the warmth moving through your arms and legs. All of your muscles relaxing and becoming more and more comfortable. Any tension that you might be holding in your neck or your back or your shoulders just drifting away,

The gentle voice over the tannoy announces the next stop, but you are not able to focus on it. It just drifts through your mind like nothing has happened. You are too comfortable now. Too relaxed. All that matters is how comfortable you feel. You take another sip of the warming tea before you settle under the blanket. You gently close your eyes and start to drift off to sleep. All you can hear as you drift off is the gentle sound of the engine and the tapping of the rain on the train roof.

4. The Sleepy Mountain (50 Minutes)

Good evening. Welcome to tonight's story. Tonight, we are going to be spending the night on the top of the sleepy mountain. One of the most relaxing places on earth. Before we begin, make sure that you are nice and comfortable. Get under the cover and close your eyes. Get into a nice comfortable position and allow any thoughts you may be having to drift away slowly. Nothing needs your attention right now. Just allow all your thoughts to come to a natural conclusion. And then bring your awareness to your breathing as you take in a deep breath and then exhale slowly. Do this a couple more times and then allow yourself to breathe normally.

Are you comfortable? Perfect. Now let's start our journey.

As you watch night drift in on the sleepy mountain, you think about how you have never seen anything so beautiful. The sky turns dark blue within seconds and it moves over you, almost like a thick blanket. It's like the world is being tucked into bed under a comfortable duvet for the night. As soon as the sky turns dark blue, you hear the birds starting to settle down for a good night's sleep. Soon their chorus ends and instead it is replaced with the sounds of crickets and the occasional hooting of a distant owl.

As you watch the sun disappear in the distant, casing one final shadow through the trees before calling it a day, you can see why this mountain is referred to as the sleepy mountain. You get the feeling that in the natural world, there are few places as comfortable and inviting as this. Few places that can make you feel so comfortable. Not just with your surroundings, but in your own skin as well. Just by looking at this place, you know that stress or feelings of anxiety do not belong here. This is a place of peace and happiness. That is why you find it so easy to just let those feelings of stress to just float away, almost like they have been caught in the mountain breeze.

When you are here on the mountain, it can feel like the whole world has gone quiet. It's almost like a quiet is descending on the whole world out of respect for what is here. The nature and sheer relaxing spirit of this place make it wonderfully unique. It is here that people often come to find serenity and peace.

Too much of our lives is dictated by work and the stresses and anxieties that come from living in the modern world. When you think of all the things that demand our attention all of the time, it's no surprising that people often find themselves overcome with feelings of stress and then develop a strong desire to take a break from it all. This sleepy mountain is the perfect place to do just that.

Here, there is no place for stress and anxiety. It would not fit into this place. That is why, as soon as you set foot on this beautiful landscape, all of those feelings simply drift away. They stop being a part of you. Instead, the mountain becomes part of you. It becomes a symbol of your happiness and how peaceful you feel in this moment.

You can see the very faint sight of car headlights in the far distance. They are coming from the road near the river down below the mountain. Even though you can see them, you cannot hear them. Normally, you would be able to hear the gentle hum of the traffic. Here, it's almost like even the cars on the road know not to disturb this place.

Even though this place is quiet, it is by no means silent. You can still hear the birds in the trees all trying to get the last word before they settle down to sleep. You can still hear the distant sound of crickets that are coming out to dance in the moonlight. The owl is still occasionally hooting in the distance. And you can hear the sound of the gentle breeze flowing through the tree branches near you. The trees sway gently in reaction to the wind, but the breeze is so gentle, it is a slight movement. The breeze is comforting against your skin. It's almost like the mountain is giving you a gift to try and help you become more relaxed. And every now and then, you can hear the sound of other night animals awakening from their day's rest.

You are sat on the deck of a beautiful log cabin. It is situated in a prime spot for you to have a glorious view over the entire mountainside. It's a magical place. Just the view alone is enough to make you feel comfortable and relaxed in your surroundings. As you look up, you can see the stars are slowly starting to appear. In the distance, where you can see a small collection of houses not far from the lake and the road, you can see some of the lights starting to come on. They shine like yellow and orange stars in the distance.

You sit back and fully take in how amazing this place is. It feels like time is almost slowing down. There is no need to rush or live life at the speed you might find in a city or bustling town. Instead, everything here goes at a calm and comfortable pace. No need to rush. No need to feel stress. All you have to do is sit back, relax and enjoy the experience of simply being here.

As you sit back on your wooden chair outside your log cabin, you can feel yourself becoming more tired. More sleepy. It's now that you know what this mountain is referred to as sleepy mountain. It is the best place in the world to simply curl up and have a peaceful night's sleep. It's like the sounds of the wind and the owls are almost serenading you as you slowly start to drift off.

This is the perfect place to come and rest after a busy day. If you ever find yourself having a stressful day where you are running around trying to deal with all the things that are demanding your attention, then I highly recommend that you end that day with a visit to the sleepy mountain. It's here that you will be able to put all of those things aside and simply enjoy having the time to yourself. A time where you can allow your mind and body to fully rest and recharge. You will be surprised just how positive an effect this place can have on you. If you visit here enough at night, you will find that you sleep comfortably through the night. And you will find that you are better equipped to deal with those stresses in life when the day comes calling.

5. The Night Sky (50 Minutes)

Hello and welcome to tonight's sleep story. As night falls, you will enter a state of rest and tranquillity as we spend some time enjoying the beauty of the night sky. So, before we begin, make yourself as comfortable as possible. Get nice and cosy under the duvet and allow the bed to support the weight of your body. Enjoy the feeling of allowing your head to rest comfortably on your pillow. And then, when you feel ready, close your eyes. Stretch out into a position where you feel like you could fall asleep.

Now turn your attention to your breathing for a moment. Take in a nice deep breath. Hold it inside for a moment and then slowly exhale. Notice how the tension is leaving your body as the air leaves. Do this a few more times, then just allow yourself to breathe normally. Allow any thoughts you may be having to come to an end. Just give your mind the space to experience clarity and stillness. Now that we are ready, we can begin our story.

It's the beginning of Summer and the evening is drawing in. It's one of those early days of summer where it still feels warm but the sun is still setting at an earlier time that it would be at the height of the season. You step out of your home and allow your front door to gently close behind you. You feel the nice gentle breeze caressing your face as soon as you step outside. It feels nice and comforting. As you start to walk, you get to fully experience how comfortable the air feels tonight. Because it is early in the Summer season, it doesn't yet feel overwhelmingly hot. The air has a nice comfortable temperature which makes walking at a steady pace feel good.

After walking for a moment, you pause and take a little moment to enjoy the feeling of being outside at this time. The streets around you are nice and quiet. It would feel like you were all alone if it wasn't for the yellow and orange glows of the windows along the street. These are the only indicators that anyone is even around. For all you know, you are the only person in the world at this moment. Just you and the gentle breeze flowing around you.

As you continue walking to the end of your street, you walk past the small garden feature at the end of your road. It's filled with daffodils and roses. It's incredible how quickly this small garden has grown over the last few months. Almost like it's had a growth spurt in excitement of what summer will bring. The plants flow gently in the breeze as you walk past. You then look at the town houses around you. Along with the yellow and orange lights streaming from the windows, you can see the occasional shadow of people settling down for the night. Enjoying the peaceful nature of the night and of the summer breeze.

As you come to the end of your street, you make a turn and start walking up the hill. Within a few minutes of walking up the cobbled road, you already feel like you're in a completely different place. You turn and look back and see all the town houses. All still emitting their orange and yellow lights. You are going somewhere where you will not be able to see those lights. The only light you will be able to see are the ones being beamed down from the night sky by the moon and the stars.

The cobbled road is steep but not too steep that's difficult to walk along. Within a few minutes you are surrounded by beautiful trees and lush vegetation. You suddenly feel so surrounded by life. In the distance, you can hear the sound of birds singing as they settle down for a good night's rest. Every now and then, you can also hear an owl hooting as it gets ready to fully experience the night.

As you reach the end of the road, you move into the trees and start following the worn, brown path that has been forged in the ground. It guides you through the trees and out into a clearing. Here the grass is nice and short and shimmering gently in the breeze. As you walk into the clearing you look up to the night sky. It's amazing how different it looks here than it did outside your home. From your door, you could see the occasional spot of light being forced through the artificial light around you. Here, there is no artificial light to disturb your view. Now you can see a huge array of stars. Just slightly to the left is the moon, shining down on your like a silver spotlight.

You sit down on the grass and continue to look up at the sky. As you take it all in, time just seems to slow down. There is nowhere else you need to be. Nothing that needs your attention in this moment. All you need to do is sit and relax and look at the amazing view of the universe you have before you. There is such an amazing array of colours coming from the stars. Some are a darker blue or a sky blue. Others are yellow and even a couple that are red. You wonder which ones are the planets in the solar system and wonder if the slightly larger, flickering red light is the sunlight bouncing off the surface of Mars.

You feel amazing during this moment. You feel so calm and at peace with yourself and your surroundings. This clearing in the middle of this field is almost like your own personal paradise. Here, there is no need to worry about things or waste your mental energy on things that might cause you stress and anxiety. All you have to do right now is sit back and fully enjoy this amazing moment.

This time is just for you and you alone. There is no one else in this clearing. Everyone else is at home settling down for that. You have this space totally for yourself to sit and look at the stars and dream about what might be out there. About the new worlds shining their warm light down on you.

You lie back on the grass. You spread your arms and legs out wide so you can get completely comfortable. It hasn't rained for a few days now so the grass feels dry and comfortable. Enjoy the feeling of being held in this place by gravity, while about you, the universe keeps rotating and expanding. All those stars looking down on you all have their own stories to tell. About how they were born millions of years ago and how they have planets circling them just like our solar system. You wonder what those planets are like. Whether they are hot or cold. Big or small. Made of gas or rock. Just allowing yourself to dream of what might be out there.

You take another look at the moon and enjoy the feeling of being able to see it shine so brightly in the sky. You can almost make out all the little details on the moon's surface. And as you are looking at it, you just slowly allow your eyes to close. You feel the wonderful breeze flowing past you. You hear the sound of the distant owl hooting as it heads out into the trees for the night. And as you are listening, you slowly allow yourself to drift to sleep. Your mind filled with wonderful, calming thoughts about all those new worlds that could be waiting for you out there in the universe.

6. A Walk Along the Canal (80 Minutes)

Good evening. Tonight, we are going to take a lovely stroll along the canal. But before we begin, make sure that you are nice and comfortable. Take a moment to get settled under the covers in a comfortable position. Then close your eyes and allow any thoughts you may be having to drift away. Enjoy the feeling of being comfortable and feeling safe and secure. Take in a few deep breaths and allow the tension to leave your body as you exhale. Enjoy this feeling. Notice how you are sinking deeper and deeper into the bed.

Are you ready? Perfect. Now we can start our walk.

The canal looks beautiful today. It's almost completely still and looks like a silky, crystal blanket. You imagine that when it is a particularly hot summer day, it would be nice to take a dip in this canal and just allow the blanket of water to wash over you. Making you feel completely comfortable and one with nature.

The water along the canal is so still it looks like glass. As you look at it, you can see the reflection of the gently moving trees behind you and on the opposite side. You take in a deep breath and enjoy the cool crispness of the air. It makes your airways feel so clear. No pollution from cars here. Just the wonderful crisp air. When you breathe out, you can almost feel the air carrying away the feelings of tension or stress you have been carrying. Just by appreciating the air by the canal, you are already feeling more comfortable and relaxed. You know that this canal is not the sort of place where you want to be carrying stress or anxiety. That's why you let it go without putting up any fight at all. Just allowing those feelings to drift away in the gentle breeze.

As you start walking, you see a tiny group of ducks making their way along the water near the opposite embankment. Up until now, it has been like you were the only living thing around. Seeing them calmly going about their day reminds you how teaming with life this area will be. How for those ducks, this blissful place is somewhere they get to call home. You watch the effects the ducks have on the water as they swim. Creating tiny ripples that move out into the canal as they get wider until they fade away.

You continue watching the ducks as they swim further and further away. Soon the only way you know they have been there is because of the remaining ripples they have left behind them on the surface of the water. On the glass-like surface, it's the only thing that has disturbed these waters. And after a moment, they go completely still again. Almost like they it has suddenly frozen in a quick frost.

As you continue to walk, you walk past an old fishing boat. Even though it has clearly been through a lot in its life, it still looks warm and inviting. You imagine what it must be like to take that boat out onto these calm waters. To just sit and fish for hours on end, just drinking tea and enjoying the calmness of the moment. You wonder if there are many fish in this canal and then you think that maybe that's not the point. Maybe just having a place where you can be totally at peace with yourself and your surroundings is all you need when you're on this boat.

The canal is so long, it seems to stretch into the horizon forever. You have only come here for a quick stroll, but the length of the canal does not bother you. If anything, you feel so relaxed that you feel like you could walk along it for hours on end. If you were still here as night drew in you would be happy. The scenery and the stillness of the canal makes you feel like you could stay here forever. You can imagine yourself walking laps of the canal for a long time. You could even see yourself just sitting on a canal boat and watching the reflections in the water. Just you and a flask of tea, watching the relexation of the sun slowly being replaced with a reflection of the moon.

When you think about the fast paced nature of life at the moment, you wonder why more people do not come to places like this. The unrelenting nature of technology and work means that many people feel like they never have a moment to switch off. Never have a moment to simply focus on being alive. And yet, you know now that places like this are exactly what you need. In this place, time is slowing down and this does not worry you. You don't feel like you have to be somewhere else or you should be thinking about other things. All you are thinking about is how beautiful this canal is and how it is helping you connect with nature. Connect with the world.

You know that you have no need to rush. There is nowhere you need to be. Nothing that needs your attention right now. If anything, you have a desire to walk a little slower along the canal. Just to give your mind and body the chance to fully embrace this experience. A chance to fully enjoy your surroundings. You know that you have all the time you need to simply breathe this all in. Just to allow any feelings of tension or stress to wash away. Almost like the ripples that you saw on the canal water surface.

There is little to no noise around you. Every now and then, you can hear the gentle ripple of the water, but even this is a faint sound. When the grass on the opposite side of you becomes long, you can hear the occasional stick insect singing. Almost like it is saying hello to you as you walk past. At this canal, you are just far enough away from civilization that you can't hear the gentle humming of cars on the road. Normally, you would be able to hear that sound in most places. But that sound doesn't belong in a place like this.

As you're walking, you notice that there is a small pub in the distance. It's on the other side of the canal and it looks warm and inviting. It has comfortable seating outside so you can sit and face the canal. You decide that you will stop there once you reach it and have a nice, cold drink. A nice chance to rest your legs for a moment and to just be still and enjoy the surroundings.

You wonder how many people must visit that pub each day. Then again, you imagine that it's quiet atmosphere and the sense of solitude that it gives you is rather the point of its existence. The landlord may well be quite happy to only have steady footfall if it means that both he and his customers get a chance to just be still and enjoy a refreshing drink in the midday sun.

As much as you are looking forward to going in the pub, you know that there is no need to rush. In this place, there is no need to hurry at all. Time has no meaning in this place. There is no need for urgency. You know that you will get to the pub eventually. But in the meantime, you can simply enjoy keep walking. Just walking and enjoying everything that the scenery has to offer.

Every now and then, you notice small birds flying around the canal. Some of them drop down to eat at small patches of moss, or attempt to dig out worms from the dusty ground. A few of them even fly and land quite close to you. They have no reason to be scared of you or your presence.

You are exuding such a calm and relaxed aura that these birds know that you will only appreciate their presence. Much like the stick insects you have passed, some of the chirp at you in a greeting as you walk past them. You smile at them in response and they look at you almost like they have registered your good nature.

As you approach the pub, you notice yet another group of ducks is making its was down the canal. You stop and watch them for a moment. You wonder if they are joining the group that you saw earlier. The swim close to the opposite side of the canal. They pass underneath the hanging trees, giving them some brief moments of shade from the sun beating down on them. They slow down as they pass under the branches, almost taking the opportunity to get as much of the shade as they can. They seem like they are almost savouring the moment.

As you watch them, you know that they don't consider the sun to be unpleasant. In fact, when they are passed the branches and they are exposed to the sunlight again, they seem quite happy to be back under the warm rays. It's simply that they are enjoying the experience of being on the canal. They like the shade just as much as they like the sunlight. Much like yourself, they simply want to take a moment and appreciate everything that this canal has to offer. They are completely free of any concerns. They can simply drift down the canal slowly and enjoy the feeling of calmness that surrounds them.

You reach the pub. You order yourself a large drink with ice and then you take a seat on one of the benches outside. You stretch your feet out and take a sip of your drink. The coolness of it fills your body, making you feel completely relaxed. You look out over the canal and then gently close your eyes. As you do, all you can hear is the sound of the canal moving gently and the birds chirping in the distance.

You take another sip of your drink now as the coolness spread around your body once more. And then, you quietly drift off, just listening to the sound of the birds and then gentle canal.

7. A Walk Through The Magic Garden (60 Minutes)

Hello and welcome to tonight's sleep story, where we will be making a visit to the Magic Garden. Before we begin, take a moment to make yourself feel nice and comfortable. Get settled under the covers and get into a position where you feel like you could fall asleep. Then when you are ready, just gently allow your eyes to close. Enjoy how it feels to shut the world out for the day. Take in some nice deep breaths and then allow the air to slowly leave your body. Enjoy the feeling of tension leaving your body. Once you feel nice and comfortable, just allow yourself to breathe normally. Now that you are comfortable, we will begin our story.

Our story begins as the sun rises over what the local villagers call the Magic Garden. As the sun rises over the stone walls that surround the edges of the garden, the warmth of the light hits the plants. They almost react in the light, like they are stretching out to start the new day. As the sun rises further, it hits the small bushes and bounces off the surface of the pond and the water in the fountain at the centre of the garden.

Tonight's story is all about Peter. Peter is the main who tends to the Magic Garden. This is something he has done since he was 18. Before that, he would help his father take care of the garden. His father had actually created the garden when he was 18 and had been taking care of it every since. Every day he would go and deal with the weeds and feed the fish in the fish pond. Peter would go with his father almost every morning from the point he turned six. He would get up extra early to go with him so he could help with the garden before school. It was his father's pride and joy. Now, it's Peter's pride and joy.

Peter has learned everything about gardening from his father. How to remove weeds without damaging the plants. What to do when foxes are disturbing the hedging. Whenever Peter needs to add new plants to the garden, he always thinks about how his dad would search for hours to find the right one. Every living thing in the garden had to be perfect.

Peter left early just like he did every morning. He closed the door of his cottage and then headed to the garden. Peter always preferred getting to the garden nice and early so then he could tend to the plants before more people arrived. Nearly every morning while walking to the garden, he would think about walking with his dad. Holding his hand as he walked and feeling so excited to get to the garden so he could start work. He would often ask his dad if the garden was actually magical. His father told him that it is magical if he believes it is. Since then, Peter has always believed deep down that it is indeed magical.

When Peter arrived that morning, he started by sweeping away the stay leaves that had blown over the cobbled paths during the night. Luckily it had been a relatively calm Spring night, so he didn't have to spend too long clearing them away. He then started filling the bird feeders in the trees, which were now starting to attract a wide array of birds. A blue tit sat on a branch nearby watching him as he filled one of the feeders. He smiled at the bird as he finished and beckoned it over. The blue tit cautiously approached and then started eating gleefully as Peter walked away.

Peter fished the leaves out of the fountain with a net. As he cleared away the few leaves that had blown in overnight, he looked at all the coins resting at the bottom of the fountain. All the wishes that had been made by children and parents. He felt like there was more coins than usual. It made him wonder if there was something in the air recently that was making people hope their wishes would come true. And he wondered if those people did truly believe the garden was magical, for he knew that if they truly believed then what they wished for would come true.

Peter watched the beautiful fountain for a moment, taking in the majesty of the falling water. Then he turned his attention to the fish pond. He ran his net over the top and removed the leaves from the surface. As he did, the fish in the pond rose to the surface, hoping that Peter has not forgotten their early morning meal. Peter reached into his bag and pulled out the fish food. The fish almost seemed to react in excitement at the sight of the bag. Peter reaches into it and pulls out a handful of food. He scatters it over the surface of the pond and the fish rush to get their breakfast. Peter watches them as they hoover up the food in short order. He feels a momentary temptation to give them more, but he knows he should not over feed them. Instead he leaves them and turns his attention back to the rest of the garden.

Peter always enjoys how the garden feels at this time in the morning. When the sun is only just coming up and the birds are singing. He can walk around the garden and enjoy the feeling of stillness it holds. He felt privileged to be one of the few people who could enjoy the garden when no one else was around. Even during heavy rain, there would still be people taking strolls through the garden, many of them appreciating how the garden seemed that little bit happier whenever there was a downpour.

He always appreciated the feeling of the cobbles under his feet. In the Summer months he would take advantage of the earlier morning sun by heading to the garden even earlier in the morning. When he had finished his jobs, he would remove his shoes and walk on the cool cobbles in his bare feet. If it had been an uncomfortably hot night, the feeling of the cobbles on his feet would be a pleasant relief.

Peter then headed to the large oak tree at the back of the garden. This was the largest tree in the garden and Peter would go and sit under it for a few minutes every morning. It was just a place where he could have five minutes to himself and enjoy the peaceful nature of the garden. He would sit cross legged and just look at the tree. Just taking in how impressive and beautiful it was. How for many it was the highlight of the garden. He would sit and watch the morning sunlight bursting through the few gaps in the branches.

He thought about the day this tree was planted. He was around eight years old and his father wanted to make improvements to the rear of the garden. Peter asked his dad if he could plant his own oak tree, the first thing he would ever plant. His father helped him prepare the earth and did the hole while Peter planted the seeds. His father then piled earth onto the seeds and made it even. Peter couldn't wait to see how big the tree would become.

When they left the garden that morning, Peter's father gave him a penny and told him to make a wish in the fountain. Peter held the coin tightly, closed his eyes and concentrated on his wish. He wanted it to come true more than anything and he knew that the garden could make it happen if he just believed. He then took in a deep breath and threw the coin into the fountain. He opened his eyes and watched the coin sink slowly down to the bottom of the fountain. When his father asked him what he wished for, Peter said he couldn't say because then it wouldn't come true. His father smiled and told him that as long as he kept his wish secret, the garden may well make the wish come true.

On this beautiful morning, Peter smiled at the memory of his father. He looked up at the beautiful oak tree and thought about how in that moment, the garden really had been magic. Peter took one last look at the oak tree. The largest tree in the garden and his pride and joy.

He then took his gardening equipment and started to leave the garden, leaving it ready for the day ahead. Peter wondered what other wishes would be made in the Magic Garden today and if any of them would become true. After all, Peter knew that if you wished hard enough, the garden really would be magic.

8. Picnic Near the Waterfall (50 Minutes)

Hello and welcome to tonight's sleep story for adults. Before we begin, make sure that you are nice and comfortable in bed. Get nice and warm under the covers. Stretch out if you can and enjoy the space you have around you. Take a moment to fully settle into a comfortable position. Become more aware of the bed supporting your body. Enjoy the feeling of the pillow gently supporting your head. Then, when you are happy, take in a nice deep breath. Hold it inside for a moment and then exhale slowly. Now gently close your eyes and allow your mind to power down. Know that this is the time to settle down and rest. End any thoughts you might be having. Just gently allow your mind to clear as you get ready for the picnic near the waterfall.

As you walk through the dense woodland towards the waterfall, you feel a great sense of excitement. You can't wait to get to the waterfall and settle down with the picnic basket you are carrying with you. For the last few days, it feels like it has been raining constantly. Every time you have looked out of your window and thought about how much you have wanted to go for a picnic, you have been repelled by the sight of dense, grey and dark clouds hanging above you. They have been sending down a hammering of rain for what feels like an eternity.

This morning however, things are different. You have awoken to the sight of a beautiful blue sky. The only clouds you have seen are thin and wispy and certainly pose no threat to the warm and inviting climate. You can tell it must have been warm overnight as the ground is completely dry. Even the grass just outside your home feels comfortable. Certainly comfortable enough to sit and lie back on, especially if you have a soft blanket helping to support you.

As soon as you saw the sky this morning, you knew that you could not waste this opportunity. You packed up your picnic basket. You filled it with your favourite sandwiches and snacks and a flask filled with tea. You grabbed a blanket and stuffed it into the basket and then ran out of the door. The state of euphoria you feel almost makes you forget to lock your door as you leave the house and head towards the woodland about half a mile from your home.

Now, you are walking through that woodland. With each step that you take, you are moving closer and closer to the waterfall. You can hear the crashing water already even though you know you still have a little further to walk. In this woodland, you can't hear any of the traffic on the motorway in the distance. You can just about see some of the cars through the gaps in the trees but the gentle humming of their engines can't seem to penetrate the trees. It's almost like the soundwaves know they would be unwelcome in this place. This is a place of tranquility and calmness. A place where people can visit and feel one with nature. A place where they can come and leave all of the worries and pressures of modern life at home.

With every step you are taking through the woodland, you can feel yourself becoming more and more relaxed. All of those things that have been bothering you or making you feel stressed in life have been left behind. You closed the door on them as soon as you left the house with your picnic basket. Right now, all you have to do is relax and enjoy your surroundings. Enjoy being in the here and now. Enjoy the woodland and wonderful sounds that nature provides. The sound of the breeze gently flowing through the gaps in the tree branches. The sound of distant birds. Some of them move closer as they sing, hopping along from tree to tree around you. The sound of their chirping almost sounds like they are greeting you to the woodland.

You can almost feel the vibrations of the waterfall in the ground now. In your mind, you can see the crashing waves as you move ever closer. The vibrations caused by the crashing water feel like they are moving through your body. It almost feels like you are being given a gentle massage. Like the waterfall is already trying to ease any feelings of tension out of your body. Any feelings of tension you might have been holding in your back or in your shoulders or neck are slowly being soothed by the vibrations. And with each step towards the waterfall you take, you can feel the vibrations getting stronger.

You enjoy the smell of the pine trees around you. As you walk, you can see small beads of water dripping down from the branches onto the dry forest floor below them. These last remnants of the rainfall are now slowly drying away. You can almost hear the small drops as they come down from the high branches, hitching rides on the branches further down until eventually they are able to gracefully make the short drop down to the gravelly ground.

Finally, as you notice the trees starting to become increasingly less dense, you emerge out into the clearing. And there in front of you is the top of the waterfall. You take a moment to fully appreciate how beautiful it looks. How comforting it is to hear the sound of the water crashing down below you. As you look down, you see the steam from the water as it impacts the stream below, before the water calms and forms a gentle lake the sweeps off into the distance.

Just by standing here, you can feel tension that you could have been holding inside of you for years slowly starting to drift away. You remember why you have come to this place and why you have been so eager to come here. This place is the home of total tranquillity. This is a place where all worries and troubles can be washed away, almost like they are being released over the edge of the waterfall. Just being allowed to slip away on the delicate stream below.

You take the blanket out of your picnic basket and gently lay it down on the grass. You sit down on the blanket and place your basket beside you. You take a moment to simply look out onto the waterfall. You can still hear the birds singing around you. You can even spot one or two of them flying gracefully over the edge of the waterfall as they move to the collection of dense trees on the opposite side of where you are sitting.

Fully take in how wonderful it feels to be here. Now lie back on your blanket so you are looking up at the clear sky. You can still see some of the dense trees swaying in the gentle breeze in the corner of your eye. You watch the few thin clouds above you move through the sky. You enjoy the feeling of the warm sun on your skin. It doesn't feel too hot. It's just right. Just enough to make you feel comfortable and to compliment the breeze perfectly.

Now, as you listen to the sound of the crashing waterfall just a few steps away from you, gently allow your eyes to close. Feel the breeze and the sunshine. Listen to the distant birds and the sound of the crashing waterfall as you slowly drift off to sleep. All the while, still fully experiencing how wonderful it is to have this time to lie back and fully enjoy the magical wonder of this gracious and breathtaking waterfall.

9. A Night On Your Paradise Island (70 Minutes)

Hello and welcome to tonight's sleep story. Tonight, we will be spending the night on your own personal paradise island. This is a place that belongs to you and you alone. So, take a moment to get nice and comfortable. Allow your mind to slow down and you get comfortable in bed. Get into a position where you feel like you could fall asleep and then allow your eyes to close. Take in a few deep breaths and then slowly release the air. Do this a few times until you notice any tension that you may be holding slowly leaving your body. Then when you feel completely comfortable, allow yourself to breathe at a normal pace. Now that you are ready and you are completely comfortable in bed, we can travel to your paradise island.

As you stand on the beach at Paradise Island, you watch the sun as it starts to set over the horizon. A blushing colour of orange and yellow bursting in the distance. Watching the ebb and flow of the waves as they gently crash against the sea, try and make your breath line up with the waves. Breathing in deeply as the water hits the shore and then breathing out as the waves retreat back into the vast ocean. Watch the waves come in and pull back again.

You appreciate the feeling of the gentle breeze as it flows around you. You take in a deep breath and savour the feeling of the sea air entering your airways. Above you, you can see the beautiful sky. It's filled with an array of colours as the day begins the transition to night. You look at the sky turning to a lighter shade of blue in the distance, where the sky is meeting the lowering sun over the distant horizon. You enjoy the feeling of the sand underneath your bare feet. You feel an amazing sense of connection with the island and indeed the world around you.

There is no one around you. No one for miles around. This is almost your own personal place. A private oasis where you can feel connected with the earth. A place to feel one with the planet and with the natural world. Away from bustling cities or a hectic workplace. Nothing but you and your surroundings.

You watch as the sun continues to set over the horizon. After a few moments, it gets replaced by the bright moon as it rises in the sky. You notice the reflection its casting into the sea, like a silver orb of light and energy. As the waves move, it's almost like the reflection is dancing on the surface of the water. You watch as stars start to come out to play for night. Soon they're filling the sky. There are so many colours. From purple to a lighter blue to a much heavier, darker blue. The moon and stars illuminate the beach. You're surrounded by their natural light as you listen to the waves continue to gently wash against the beach.

You take in a deep breath. You feel more and more relaxed in these surroundings. Your connection with Paradise Island is making you feel more happy. As a reaction, your entire body starts to relax. The muscles in your head and your face. Your jaw starts to loosen. Any tension in your chest and stomach just drifting away. All the muscles in your arms and your legs become heavy and relaxing. The only thing you are aware of now are your feet. Your feet as they connect you to the sandy beach. As they connect you to the earth and the pure nature around you.

You take a moment to simply observe your breathing. Notice the warm sea air filling your lungs. And then as you breath out, the sea carries away any tension or stress you may be feeling. Once again you try and match your breathing with the movement of the waves. You take in a nice deep breath as the waves hit the sandy beach. And then you breathe out as the water slowly retreats back into the vast ocean. While you're doing this, you continue to take in the beauty of the stars and the moon. You watch as their light dances on the surface of the ocean. They're illuminating the night with their calming energy.

You turn around and take in the rest of the island. All you can hear is the soft waves hitting the beach as you watch the palm trees. They are blowing gently in the cool sea breeze, almost like a gentle swaying. As you walk further into the island, you start to notice the sound of crickets as well, almost joining the waves and the breeze in a chorus of songs.

You notice how the palm trees all look so strong and stable. You touch one of them as you walk past and you can almost feel the energy from the tree being passed into your body. A calming energy that is making you feel more relaxed.

You feel completely safe as you walk deeper into the island. You feel like nothing can disturb you during this moment. You are experiencing pure calmness and relaxation. During this moment of oneness, you feel completely connected with the world around you. And you have been able to find this wonderful feeling through the power of your own mind. This is your personal place. No one can disturb you here.

Stop walking for a moment and sit down on the ground. You cross your legs and sit with your back resting against the tree. You look up at the stars and you feel like this is the first time you have really seen the stars. The first time you have really taken in how far away there are. How vast the universe is and what a gift it is to be a living being in the middle of the miracle of creation.

The sounds of crickets and birds join in to form a chorus with the sound of the waves. You enjoy listening to these sounds as they fill the night air. You take in another deep, relaxing breath and fill your lungs with sea air. As you breathe out, you release those last bits of tension in your body as you get back to your feet and continue walking deeper towards the heart of the island.

You feel fully present while you are here. Like you only exist in this current moment and nothing else matters. You feel a warmth inside you and a happiness. And you know that really, this is how you should feel most of the time. This is how human beings should feel. They should feel calm and appreciative of the world around them. And they should be able to fully enjoy moments like this.

As you move through the trees, you come to a lovely, tranquil pond. You take a moment then you decide to climb into the pond. You enjoy the feeling of the cool and comforting water as it washes over your skin. Even the nights are quite warm on your paradise island, so having this place to cool down feels very welcome. You enjoy the feeling of the water on your skin as you move deeper into the water. You keep moving until nearly your entire body is submerged. You take a moment to fully enjoy the cool sensations washing over you. It's almost like you are being held by a nice thin blanket as you settle down to enjoy the warm evenings that this personal paradise has to offer.

You kick your legs back and allow yourself to start floating on the surface of the pond. All you can see above you is the night sky as you start drifting down the pond. You enjoy the feeling of weightlessness. It's almost like you are a feather floating on a gentle breeze.

You continue to float down the pond now as you look up again to the night sky. You take in the beauty of it as the crickets and the birds continue with their evening songs. As you float further and further down the pond, the sound of the waves become more and more distant.

You enjoy the embrace of the water. You feel like you can let go of everything you have been holding on to. You let go of any stresses or worries. You let go of any bad feelings you have about others or yourself. You let it all go as it all sinks to the bottom of the pond while you continue to float.

As you reach the edge of the lake, you climb onto the side and lie down. You continue looking up at the night sky as you allow the warm air to slowly dry your skin. You can still feel the cool feelings of the water settling into your skin. Sinking deeper even to your muscles. You close your eyes and enjoy the feelings moving slowly through your body right now. All you can hear now is the sound of the birds and crickets as they serenade you through the night as you slowly drift off to a relaxing and rejuvenating sleep.

10. A Trip Down the River (60 Minutes)

Hello and welcome to tonight's sleep story. Tonight, we are going to go on a nice calming trip down the river. But before we do, it's important that we are nice and comfortable for the journey. So, get nice and comfortable under the covers. When you are ready, close your eyes and just allow the bed to support your body. Allow your head to sink into the pillow. Just allow your body to rest and begin the process of recharging. Take in some deep breaths and then allow the air to slowly leave your body. Imagine that the air you are breathing out is carrying any tension that you feel you might be holding in your muscles. Then, once you have done this a few times, simply breathe normally. Now, we will begin our journey.

The river is always an amazing place to visit at night. Many people say that this river in particular is good to visit. Many say that if you go during the daylight hours, you're not going to get the full effect of the river and the life that inhabits along its banks until you go at night. It's then that the river truly comes to life and you can fully experience what it has to offer.

The flowers along the banks all look calm and content. The sunflowers are all huddled together, almost like the are snuggling up for a comfortable night's sleep. Other flowers around all have thick, green stalks, like they are braced for any sort of change in the elements over the course of time. Just by looking at them, you can see that they have been around for a while and that they are prepared for anything. It would take more than a strong wind or a heavy downpour of rain and hail to break their spirits. Even if you were stood their in the worst of snowstorms, these flowers would still all be standing defiantly tall. Undisturbed by the elements as they carried on with their lives.

As you walk along the bank, you notice that some of the other flowers are moving more strongly in the breeze. As you listen to the trickle of the water as it moves down the river, you wonder if the flowers are actually dancing in response to the rhythmic sounds. Some of the sunflowers along the side are drooping their heads lower, almost like they are trying to reach down and take a sip from the flowing water.

As you continue walking, you notice a thick tree trunk that has fallen into the river. It's clearly been there for some time. For many places, the sight of a fallen tree would be a bad thing. But here, the river has seen an opportunity to make something beautiful. Over the years, the river has helped make the tree trunk part of the impressive scenery. Moss has started to grow over the trunk to form a comfortable green carpet. You notice a couple of frogs have jumped onto the log and seem to be enjoying the comfort of the moss under their webbed feet. It's admirable how this place has even been able to take something like the death of a tree and turn it into an opportunity to create a unique characteristic for itself. Something that the animals and plants alike on this river will be able to experience and enjoy.

As you continue to walk, you can see more of the trees in the distance. As you look further ahead, you can see where the river slopes off into the dense woodland. Even though you are far away from this part of the river, you can still hear the animals that live along its banks. The birds are finishing their days of singing and are beginning to settle down for the night. You can also hear the owls that are hooting good morning to the river as they get ready to start their night.

On the opposite side of the river, you can see the apple trees along the banks. During the summer months, children frequently come here and pick the apples from the trees. Anyone who has ever eaten an apple from one of these trees says that they are the best they have ever tasted and that it's the air and the quality of the soil around the river that give the apples such an amazing flavour. Right now, there are a collection of green and red apples hanging invitingly down from the branches. Some of them seem quite low down to the floor, almost like the trees are mindful of small children who might not be able to reach some of the apples on the higher branches.

As you look above, you can see the stars and the moon have finally come out to begin their evenings. When they come into view, they illuminate your path. The moon shimmers down on the river, almost like a spotlight. And when it does, you can see some of the fish still swimming around beneath the surface. You can see only a couple of first, but then you see a large group travelling upstream together. You watch them as they delicately sway against the current. They're not moving very fast, but then again, nothing needs to move fast in this place. By this river, time can simply come to stop and everything is okay.

As you start to think about how magical it would be to bring a boat down this river and sit on the deck, drinking tea from a flask and wrapped in a warm blanket, you can feel any stresses or worries you may have been having slowly drifting away. That is how powerful this river can be. Here, there is no need to feel stress. There is nothing commanding your immediate attention. All you have to do is relax and become one with the nature and wonderful life around you.

You continue thinking about how wonderful it would be to take a boat down here. How you could take pictures of all the plants and animals as you float by. You could get a closer look at the frogs that were on the fallen tree. You know that they would not be spooked by your presence. You can tell that they would be more than happy to see you and would feel comfortable with you around.

You see some stepping stones over a more shallow part of the river. You use them to get to the other side and when you do, you decide you must know about the truth about those apples. You decide to pick a red one from one of the branches. It shines like a jewel and you can almost see the reflection of the stars on its skin. You take one bite and as you do, you can already tell that those people were right all along. It's so juicy and full of flavour. As you swallow your mouthful, it almost feels like the apple is making your body feel more relaxed and calm. You take another bite and you notice that your muscles are releasing their tension. Some of the tension you are releasing feels like something that you have been holding inside of yourself for a long time. It feels wonderful to finally be able to let it go. Almost like you have thrown it into the river and are now watching it slowly float away.

You take a moment to just simply stand and listen to the sound of the wind flowing through the trees. Along with the sound of the owls and the movement of the river, it feels like you're being serenaded. And as the crickets start to join in for a peaceful chorus, you allow yourself to drift off to sleep. Have a nice peaceful sleep now, knowing that you can come back and have another trip down the river whenever you want.